A Present Help

Robert A. Wallace

THE UNITED CHURCH PUBLISHING HOUSE
1988

Dedication

I dedicate this book to my five children

DOLLY LANSDOWNE

BRENDA ALLEN

CRAIG WALLACE

SCOTT (TJ) WALLACE

MARK WALLACE

They have been the subjects
of some of the material and objects of the
delivery of most of it.

ISBN 0-919000-44-4

Publisher: *R. L. Naylor*
Editor-in-Chief: *Peter Gordon White*
Graphic Designer: *Marilyn James*

This book is set in Times, 10 on 12pt.

Introduction

This volume was generated by a request from the United Church of Canada for a book of short devotionals for use in church groups. These have been designed for persons who are asked, on short notice, to lead in a period of worship. They can be taken from the shelf and used with a mimimum of preparation on the part of the leader.

Here, then, are fifty-six services of worship, one for each week of the year and four for special occasions. They follow the annual cycle of group activity that commences in September and ends in August.

They are prepared having in mind all ages, both sexes, and ten provinces.

Small group meetings through the week were what I had in mind, but any worshipping group might find them helpful. A senior residence without regular professional leadership in worship could be a case in point.

Ministers may find them a worship resource. Although they are pre-pared with groups in mind, they can easily be adapted to personal devotion.

A Guide to Use
1. The resources are designed with a twenty minute period in mind. They can be abbreviated if the leader is able to take some time to do so.

2. Hymns and scripture readings are suggestions only and the leader should feel at liberty to modify them.

3. There is little variation or innovation. These resources are designed to be "surprise free", so those using them can know what to expect and can prepare easily and swiftly.

My thanks to my wife, Gwynneth, who has assisted me in gathering worship resources and who offered helpful suggestions as this volume took shape.
I am grateful to congregations in five provinces and one state who have joined with me in worship. Their support and appreciation underlie this volume.

How Much Are You Worth?

Call

Unless the Lord build the house they labour in vain who build it. Unless the Lord watches over the city the watchman stays awake in vain.

Prayer

Almighty God, you draw us into a reality deeper and broader than we have known, more satisfying than we can imagine, more compelling than we can stand without your strength, so open our minds to your new truth, open our hearts to your creative compassion and open our hands in willingness to serve, through Christ our Lord. Amen.

Scripture Reading

2 Thessalonians 3:6-13   Luke 12:1-8

Suggested Hymns

168 (possible tune 166), 161

What are you worth? If you were asked that question seriously, what would you answer?

Most people if they answered at all might estimate their financial assets. Is that how we measure our worth as a person? or anyone else's worth?

Mark Twain commented that in Boston they ask, "How much does he know?"; in New York, "How much does he make?"; and in Philadelphia, "Who were his parents?" Someone added, and in Toronto, "Where does he live?"

Looking at the light side of the question, esssayist Calvin Trilling notes a recent incident in which a man was kidnapped in the Bronx. The kidnappers demanded 100,000 dollars in ransom but his wife managed to talk them down to 30,000. She paid it and the husband arrived home unharmed. Trilling wonders, how did the man feel when he discovered he had become a discount special? Did he imagine his wife discussing him as she might a cantaloupe saying, "A hundred grand for that! the way he's going soft around the edges. I'll give you thirty. No more." Might he always wonder if thirty had been her rock bottom price?

How much are we worth? Most of us measure ourselves in usefulness which can be turned into earning power. As a French essayist said, "If you aren't rich you should always look useful". How does one measure up, then, when unemployed, or retired?

Here is another of those great shining Christian truths that we so easily take for granted. We are worth an infinite amount, each of us, simply because we are well loved children of God. Ethel Waters could always bring tears to the eyes of those who knew anything of her when she sang, *His Eye is on the Sparrow*. Her own background had been so deprived that she had come as close as any human being to being discounted like a common housesparrow. Luke says, "Are not five sparrows sold for two farthings?" Buy four and get one free. Although it has no commercial value it is not outside God's love.

The short saying about sparrows is a

6

towering affirmation. Its conviction about the infinite worth of the individual makes it a foundation stone for human rights. The long struggle for justice and mercy is strengthened by this image.

We are not valuable because of any contribution we make. We are objects of God's love simply because we are God's own. God loves us even when the investment of love brings no returns.

One of John Steinbeck's best works is the sequel to *Cannery Row, Sweet Thursday*. It is the story of the girls at the Bear Flag brothel. In that unlikely setting the reader encounters human sensitivity that is often very tender. Suzy, a country girl, is preparing for her first real date. Fauna, the madame, is preparing her. "I guess you're about ready now," Fauna says. "Is there anything I can do for you, Fauna?" "Yes, I want you to repeat after me, 'I'm Suzy and nobody else." She does. "I'm a good thing." "I'm a good thing." "There ain't nothing like me in the whole world." "There ain't nothing - aw, Fauna, now my eyes'll be red!" "They look pretty that way". Fauna, in her own strange world has recognized God's gift of uniqueness to each person. This the measure of our worth.

But now the paradox. Though each of us is of infinite worth simply because we are God's, because we are loved we do produce. We know that we'll not be loved more if we do, or loved less if we don't but we want to be worthy of that love. We want to share the plan and purpose of one who loves us so. We begin, then, with what God does for us and end with what he does in us, through us. To know the love of God is to participate in that love and its expression.

Prayer
Oh God, whose dwelling is the light of seting suns, and the round earth, and the full rich air of an autumn morning, how can our lips express our heart's joy? We have known the wonder of your gift-giving through the night, in the warmth of blankets and the comfort of a loving partner. We have wakened to the laughter of children and the sharing of the breakfast table. We have come through the green and gold of this mellow season, and we have arrived to the greetings of familiar faces and friendly handclasps after a summer of separation. We are grateful for all these your gifts and pray that as we commence a new year of activity we may do so in company with Jesus Christ, our Master and Lord, our Guide and Friend. We pray for our church in all its life and pray that you will make us worthy members of it. Through Christ our Lord. Amen.

Notes on use of this service, including dates, occasions and possible changes.

Beginnings

Call
Grace and peace be to you from our Lord Jesus Christ and from God our Creator and from the Spirit, the Nourisher.

Prayer
God of all beginnings, be present among us now, to direct our minds in the way of your purposes, to strengthen our wills in the direction of your paths, to deepen our spirits in the pursuit of justice and mercy, peace and harmony, for Christ's sake. Amen

Scripture Reading
Genesis 1:1-8   John 1:1-5

Suggested Hymns
306, ·142

A recent fall magazine cover pictured a common experience. It features a summer cottage scene. The beach is empty, the clothesline is empty save for a few clothespins. The last flowers are drooping in the garden. The stillness is almost audible. The summer is over. Many have felt the poignancy of that scene watching it through the rear view mirror this month. Every beginning begins with an ending. A new year in the life of our church begins this month, but only because the summer has ended. That ending means possibilities for new beginnings. Here we are at one of those possibilities now.

God obviously has a strong sense of beginnings. The first words in the Bible are, *"In the beginning ..."* The first words of the gospel according to John, probably the best loved book of the Bible, are the same. The Bible attaches great importance to beginnings, but they do not always come easily.

Chaim Potok in his novel, In the Beginning, opens with the thought, *"All beginnings are hard. ... I say it to myself today when I stand before a new class at the beginning of a school year ... Teaching the way I do it is particularly hard, for I touch the raw nerves of faith, the beginnings of things. Often students are shaken. I say to them what was said to me, 'Be patient. You are learning a new way.... All beginnings are hard'"*.

So we begin a new season of activity together. It is good to see old friends again. The air is mellow, and the mornings misty. There is a warm feeling in the oranges and reds of the fall. Department stores are advertising for part-time help for Christmas and the Board meets Tuesday to look at the year ahead. Beginnings give us strangely mixed feelings of anticipation and uneasiness.

Each asks, "What will my role be this year? Am I ready to commit to new responsibilities?" The New Testament recognizes our problems with new beginnings in the familiar story of the Wedding Banquet. Although the difficulty in responding is treated sympathetically, the final point of the story is that those who miss the banquet have paid too dearly for their hesitation. As we hear the story we may recall Paul's admonition "Behold, now is the acceptable time; behold, now is the day of salvation". We reply, "I must first count the cost". We are on good scriptural grounds! But scripture does not suggest that we must first, second and third count the cost!

So we remember the banquet, and the invitation unheeded. We remember, also, the story of the mustard seed. From small beginnings God has worked his will. One thing that makes us different, as Christians, is the way we deal with beginnings. The difference lies in the fact that the Christian never embarks on a project *alone*. We are confident that when we respond to the inner urgings of the spirit that we are made one with God's own love of beginnings.

In ancient cultures, when a member of the community was ill the shaman would read over him or her the story of the tribe's beginnings, the ancient myths of creation. This act indicated faith that God 's own strength still lay in new starts. What was looked for in healing was not a repair so much as a rebirth, a new life. So we too, trust that our beginnings are the start of a new life.

We listen for the inner voice bidding us to act, and then we put aside our hesitation and respond to God's nudging. In the response the energy comes. Grace always comes in transit, along the way. Our part is simply to begin. A Greek sage declared, "He has half the deed done who has made a beginning." New beginnings make new life.

Prayer
Lord God of wind and weather, Tender Shepherd of the souls of each of us, Strong Rock in stormy times, Light in the darkness, Love at our returning, we worship you and open our hearts to you for warmth and correction and direction. Bless us now with the presence of your Christ, that his words and works, his powerful presence, might fill our lives with meaning and with joy. We ask it in his name. Amen.

Notes on use of this service, including dates, occasions and possible changes.

9

Continuing

Call

We will bless the Lord at all times. His praise shall continually be in our mouths. O magnify the Lord with me, and let us exalt his name together.

Prayer

Lord God, we come adoring you, for you have come into our lives in surprising and unexpected ways. You have also come as you promised in the words and works, and the risen presence of our Lord. Come now in word and song, in scripture and hymn, in strength and in the tender whisper within. Speak to us and direct us, through Christ our Lord. Amen.

Scripture Reading

1 Corinthians 15:51-58
Matthew 13:31-35

Suggested Hymn

377, 275 (possibly use 171 as tune)

"I am the God of Abraham Isaac and Jacob". This is a familiar formula. Abraham we know about, that towering figure of faith. Jacob, "the Trickster" is one of the most colourful characters in the Bible. Isaac, however, is an obscure personality for most of us. Yet he is, in many ways, more like us than are the other two. Abraham is a quarterback, Jacob a pass receiver, but Isaac is a linebacker who holds tight while the heroes do the work.

Like most of us, Isaac could easily go unnoticed. The Bible moves from sto-

ries of Abraham with Isaac simply as the son, to stories of Jacob with Isaac simply the father. Even his wife Rebecaa is a more notable character than he.

Isaac was almost sacrificed alive by his father (imagine the life-long trauma of that!!). He was caught in a crossfire of jealousy between his mother, Sara and his father's concubine, Hagar,which resulted in his half- brother being banished. His own children quarreled and were alienated from one another and from him. In his old age he was deceived by his wife and son and he gave away all he had to the wrong child. Still he kept faith. Isaac is not so much a man of faith as he is a man of faithfulness. Jesus understood people like Isaac. He spoke a lot about holding on. "If you continue in my word you are my disciples and you will know the truth... "By your endurance you will gain your lives". Paul echoes him,"Be ye steadfast, enduring".

Few would deny the need for endurance in human accomplishment. You've got to be able to "hang in". Hosea described failure in vivid terms, "Your love is like the morning cloud - like the dew that goes early away." That could make us wince! Endurance is not very exciting. One might prefer insight, intelligence, gallantry or charm.

The disciples' capacity for endurance was not too impressive. One of the most haunting lines in the New Testament is "Could you not watch with me one hour?" Before they were through, however, the disciples had learned some important lessons about endurance, about continuing.

They had learned that God accepted them despite their limitations. For those first followers the commitment to faith was a costly one. Like Christians in East Bloc countries today, it meant forfeiting advancement. Christians in North America today may experience a little scorn or condesension, the odd invitation withheld, but not much more. Still, the daily drudgery of doing good can overwhelm us on occasion. The faith journey is no Concorde flight to the Kingdom of God, but a slow march over long years with poor equipment.

Our faith is fractional, our vision blurred, our victories always incomplete, God knows. But that is precisely the point. God knows, God understands. We are not Gods, but we are children of God, and well-loved children. It is this assurance that allows us to listen to the poet Rilke when he says, "Be patient towards all that is unresolved in your heart and try to love the questions themselves."

The disciples also learned that they could push themselves more than they had known. One church member recalls her mother's adage "Always hoe to the end of the row" Hoeing in the hot sun is a tough job. Some works of love and compassion are just as hard, and tiring, and with no visible reward.

When the Canadian hockey team brought home the Canada Cup in 1987 Mike Keenan, the coach, pointed to the importance of the support cast who worked behind the stars. "It was the muckers and grinders who came through". Sports jargon, always colourful, conveys here the feelings of tedium and fatigue.! "Muckers and grinders". Most of us feel that way about ourselves. We can trust that God is at least as appreciative as a hockey coach.

Muckers and grinders are those who stay with it. A healthy soul is one that is on the grow. A healthy congregation is one that is always under construction.

James J. Braddock, heavyweight champion of many years ago, said, "When your nose is bleeding and your eyes are black and you are so tired you wish your opponent would crack you one on the jaw and put you to sleep, fight one more round - remember, the person who fights one more round is never whipped."

Prayer

God, we are grateful for the beauty of this season, for the swift kaleidescope of autumn that surprises us each morning with new colours. the air of anticipation that makes the new season pregnant with possibility, the excitement of a new dimension of living in family and church. May we make good use of these new possibilities never forgetting in our weariness and discouragement that you are our strength and our stay. Amen.

Notes on use of this service, including dates, occasions and possible changes.

Holy Ground

Call

O Lord, how manifold are your works. In wisdom you have made them all. The earth is full of your creatures. May the glory of the Lord endure for ever and may the Lord rejoice in his works.

Prayer

Lord God, we come out of a demanding and busy life into the calm and quiet of your presence. Still our minds, soothe our spirits, and hold us in the hollow of your hand, that we may return to our day, refreshed by this time in your presence, renewed by the healing of your sprit, and enlivened by your own purposes for our days. In Jesus name, Amen.

Scripture Reading

Isaiah 6:1-8   Exodus 3:1-10

Suggested Hymns

9, 197

In each part of Canada fall casts its spell over the earth. For some it will mean the sun breaking through to set a hillside of sumac aflame; for some "the rich ripe tint of the cornfields and the wild geese flying high"; and for others the impossible oranges and reds of the maple sugars in full regalia.

Martha Williams, an Iowa homemaker, writes,

God, today there's been no time to talk,
No minute to meditate, no hour to pray,
But,
I have glimpsed your robe
Among the golden leaves around the kitchen door;
I learned the cost of your concern
As my son skipped off to school;
I shared with you my neighbours cup,
Coffee filled, problem brimmed.
I worked with, you
In weary wonder sorting big red apples.
God, do you set September's bush aflame
Calling us anew to find holy ground?

Martha Williams found "holy ground" much as Moses did. We know we are on holy ground when we sense life invaded by another dimension. We are tripped out of the ordinary into the extraordinary and find ourselves in the dazzling presence of God.

It is what the theologian Rudolf Otto called "the numinous". We feel awe and wonder, something close to "the fear of the Lord". We are drawn near yet forced to our knees. We turn aside. We take off our shoes. This is holy ground.

We are drawn to the mystery of it. Mystery is not a puzzle. Puzzles have solutions. But with mystery, the more understanding the deeper the mystery. Ask anyone in love.

The mystery may come in church. "In the year that King Uzziah died, I saw the Lord high and lifted up and his train filled the temple." In worship we are often caught up by the presence of God and are lifted to one who is King of Kings, and Lord of Lords. Kenneth Clark talks of the cathedrals of Europe where "they could make stones seem weightless; the weightless expression of the spirit". Yet even the humble frame church can house the weightless spirit of God. We can share Isaiah's vision of God so high and lifted up that we are like grasshopper's around his feet.

So, with Moses, we turn. Moses' story, like every Biblical account of meeting God, is played out on a dimly lit stage, full of shadows and depths. It is not a nice neat set of propositions like an account book or a driver's manual. Life at its richest and deepest poses more questions than it answers.

Moses' story - and Isaiah's - and Martha Williams' - end as every valid experience of the presence of God ends, with new responsibility. "Go to Pharoah - tell him to let my peole go." "Whom shall I send?" And I said, "Here am I send me." "Calling us anew".It would be so much easier if we could simply bask in the presence, if we could just let God soak us up into himself. Old Testament and New are joined in the consistent conviction that there is no encounter without demand. There is healing - and joy - and peace - and demand always. No cross, no crown.

From encounter to awe, from awe to wonder, from wonder to new responsibility, - this is the pattern of God's dealing with us all.

Prayer

God - Creator of mimsts and mellow fruitfulness, how great you are! When we watch the earth put on its autumn garments, gold and brown, we know that you have come to the time for plucking up what is planted, a time to rest. We are awed by the wisdom of the seasons. As we feel the life of our towns and cities gather speed, we realize that you have made us to live in community, and we are grateful for the mutuality you have written into human life. As we waken in our homes and begin another round of activity we bless you for those we love and who love us and we acknowledge you as parent of us all. As we gather in this fellowship, we are caught up into the communion of saints, those who have worshipped you through all time and in all places. We hear the echo of their voices singing "Alleluiah" through the arches of the years. We feel the tug of those ties that bind us to all your children. We thank you for the presence of Jesus Christ, the one for all seasons, whose glorious example, whose strong words, whose warm and living presence, enriches all of life. Open our ears and our hearts to his leading this week and to the wonder of your presence with us through each day. We ask it in Christ's name. Amen.

Notes on use of this service, including dates, occasions and possible changes.

O Promise Me

Call

What shall we give to the Lord for all he has given us? We shall thank him and acknowledge him before all people.

Prayer

We confess to you, O Lord, that we are not the people we would like others to think we are. We are afraid to admit even to ourselves what lies in the depths of our souls. Yet we know we cannot hide our true being from you. You know our inner being; still you love us. Grant us, then, your forgiveness and cleansing, we pray, and grant us also the assurance of your presence always, through Christ our Lord., Amen.

Scripture Reading
Acts 3:36-47

Suggested Hymns
304, 323

All the deepest and richest moments in life involve promises; baptism, confirmation, weddings, the sacraments.

"O Promise Me" was once a popular song at weddings. It is not so now. The words are a bit sentimental for a cooler generation. A wedding is certainly filled with promises. "Will you love , comfort, honour and keep , - in sickness and in health, in joy and in sorrow?" These are big promises.

"Do you promise to raise these children in the knowledge and the love of God?" "I, John, take you, Mary". "We here offer and dedicate ourselves ...". We are never the same persons again after we have made such solemn promises.

The couple who run to the car through the shower of confetti will never be the same people who entered the church separately just minutes before.

The birth of a child means for the parents an end to one style of life, for they become new persons as much as the child is a new person. "All you who do truly and earnestly repent" are expected to "walk in newness of life".

Some professions lean heavily on promises. When a lawyer hands you a card and says, "I give you my undertaking in this matter", she is making a powerful promise. A business person who signs a "promissary note" has undertaken serious responsibility. A Boy Scout or Girl Guide is impressed with the "Promise"that must be renewed at each gathering.

Promises do change us. There are a few sacred promises which, when made, determine the persons we will be for the rest of our lives. The person becomes the promise. The mezzusah in a Jewish home, the small scroll and container, mounted in the doorway, touched each day as people pass in and out, is a reminder of promises to God. Tom Dooley, doctor to the poor of Asia, kept going till he died of cancer at a young age, saying, "I have promises to keep."

There is nothing quite so sad as the abject disappointment of a child who says, "But you promised..." Yet we do break promises - because we are frail, because the promise was ill-considered, because we were less than honest from the start. Parents do fail children, and children parents. Marriages break up and loyalties break off, and high intentions break down.

One church member, feeling uneasy about congregational promises at Baptism, wrote her minister. "I have two questions. l)Is a promise to which we have been given the answer in advance really of value? 2) Are we not giving the message that promises made in church are largely impossible, irrelevant and not to be taken seriously?

The congregation's promises are ambitious. Obviously most church members are not individually going to provide the sort of support that godparents are, much less the support that parents give. The member will not teach the child grace at meals, read stories with powerful values, tuck in and kiss goodnight with prayer, or bury the pet dog. But behind the congregation's promise is the desire to create a community of faith that will back the parents and godparents in such practises.This is a "corporate" promise from the Body of Christ, to be "the church in your life" for this family. This is accomplished best by remaining true to the promises made at membership.

Tennyson writes, "Live pure, speak truth, right wrong,/Follow the King,/ Else wherefore born?"
The huge Young's Concordance with large pages and tight-packed print gives one full page of texts where the word "promise" is used. Just as one would expect! Every single text refers to God's promises - not ours! "For the promise is to you and your children". Our grandparents used to sing about "Resting on the promises of God.". When we make our promises they are swept up into the powerful promises of God. And in that fact lies our confidence to make the promises we do.

Prayer
Oh Jesus, we have promised to serve you to the end. We have made other promises that depend on this one. We so easily slip away from all that we have promised but when we stand before you the memory of them brings us to remorse and to fresh determination. Grant us courage to recall the depth of our promising that we may know the need to renew them before you this day. We pray in the name of him who promised to be with us always, even to the end. Amen.

Notes on use of this service, including dates, occasions and possible changes.

Its a Small World

Call
What shall I render to the Lord for all his benefits to me? I will lift up the cup of salvation and call upon the name of the Lord.

Prayer
Almighty God, unto whom all hearts are open, all desires known, and from whom no secrets are hid, cleanse the thoughts of our hearts by the inspiration of your Holy Spirit, that we may love you and magnify you now and forever, Amen.

Scripture Reading
Acts 17: 22-31

Suggested Hymns
273, 337

When Dr. Bruce MacLeod was Moderator of the United Church of Canada he often surprized, amused and pleased his audiences by walking over to a nearby piano and leading the whole group in singing a hymn or song. One of his favorites was "Its a Small World After All." He might have been speaking about the local situation for a time, and then gone on to talk about the national church and finally concluded with some comments on the world church as he had seen it. By the time he had finished it did seem like a small world and his hearers could sing with conviction.

Some of you may have heard the song while sailing through Disneyland or Disneyworld. A trivial tune , maybe, with oversimple ideas about the world, yet the words tell a truth. It is a small world and becoming smaller daily. One has only to compare the possibilities of world travel for any of us to those of our grandparents. We are aware of the whole world in a way that no one could have been without those first photographs of planet earth taken from Mariner I. A recent issue of *En Route*, the Air Canada magazine, told of how the financial world had changed because, with the touch of a computer button, world markets shift and every nation is effected.

TV documentaries occasionally present a people in some remote part of the Amazon valley or New Guinea who are unaware of any world beyond the mountains that surround their villages. In a recent one an anthropologist who had been observing a tribe said "They live as humane loving families but that feeling extends only to the tribe. Anyone outside their own tribe is as open to attack as an animal.They do not see themselves as part of a species - the human".

Not long ago in human history this attitude was the norm. It was Rome that first pulled the peoples of the western world into an empire that recognized all humans as part of one family. Rome created the human family for the west, but theirs' was an intellectual concept. It was Jesus Christ who gave the notion its heart. He came with the revolutionary message of the family of humankind. Each person is a child of the God who has no only children. "He has made of one blood all the nations on the earth."

It is a simple song with a simple message, but putting the message to work is a lifelong task. The message must get from the head to the heart before it can effect the way we deal with people day to day.

A young man was visiting the home of a friend whose grandfather was a retired, elderly minister. After supper the older man retired to one corner of the room near a reading lamp. There he sat with a large atlas in his hands, seeming to read, his lips moving slightly, but with his eyes closed. "What is he doing?" whispered the visitor. "He's praying." "But how come the atlas?" "He doesn't want to miss anyone!"

Each of us will have people around the world who come to our minds on World Wide Communion Sunday or through the week that precedes or follows.((You may want a quiet time in which the group bring people to mind))

The brotherhood, sisterhood, the family of God, children of God, - these phrases come easily. We nod in agreement. They are not easy to live by when the pinch comes. Self-interest is more subtle for us than for the Indian in the Amazon valley, but it is also more far-reaching. We have more to lose.

Still we have caught a glimpse of the richness of family life in diverse national groupings. Sisterhood, brotherhood, will be real only when we meet in the flesh, when we take time to enter into the lives of those whose backgrounds are different to our own. Its small world after all. That may cause fear - it can also cause rejoicing. Let's ((hear it or sing it-whichever you prefer))

Its a world of laughter,its a world of tears,
Its a world of hope, and a world of fears,
There's so much that we share, that its time we're aware, its a small, small world.
Its a small world after all, its a small world after all,
Its a small world after all, its a small, small, world.

Prayer

Keep our eyes on distant horizons, O God. May we see and care for a world that suffers and yearns for peace. We pray for victims of oppression, but also for the oppresssors. We pray for the hungry and for those who exploit them. We pray for the ill and the weary around the world. In the turmoil of national rivalries and in civil unrest we pray that you will bring peace, for without you there can be none. We pray for leaders faced with impossible demands on their time and spirit, peoples faced with hopelessness, ancient enemies who would sooner die together than live together. We pray for all whose homes and hearts are broken by war or the threat of war. In Jesus' Name. Amen.

Notes on use of this service, including dates, occasions and possible changes.

Split Level Thanksgiving

Call

You are our God and we will give you thanks; you are our God and we will extol you. We will give thanks to you O Lord, for you are good, for your steadfast love endures for ever.

Prayer

All great God, in whom are contained all gifts and grace, all treasures and discovery; open our eyes in this time that we might behold the wonders of your love in your word and your world. Give us grace to perceive behind the gifts the Giver and so choose freely to follow you in whom all good exists. Amen.

Scripture Reading

Psalm 139:13-18
2nd Corinthians 4:5-11; 16-18

Suggested Hymns

386, 383

Life, like music, is written on two levels. Music has a treble line and a bass line, marked by the two distinctive clefs. The bass line is the "bottom line" of earth-bound realities, seen, touched and heard. This is the totally human side of life and it can be good or bad, light or heavy, happy or gloomy.

The treble line is what philosophers call "the transcendent", the divine reality that now and then breaks in on us, sometimes to judge, sometimes to inspire. It is the glory that now and then erupts in the midst of the commonplace, lighting up life for a moment with an unearthly splendour. It is a gift of God. It is no less real than the bass line.

Life is most real when the piece that was originally written for two hands brings the two melodies together in haunting harmony like the modern Christmas carol, "God above, man below; holy is the life I know."

The church year comes with the sound of the two lines. Advent has both promise and threat in the angel's message to Mary. Christmas itself tells of a lonely delivery far from home but there are angel voices singing an anthem above Bethlehem. Epiphany brings the wise men with a faraway look in their eyes and exotic gifts in their packs, but it brings, as well, the threatening plots of Herod. Lent emphasizes the tough, lean muscular discipline of Christian living while, at the same time, promising a renewel of spirit to those who are willing to follow Christ's way. Good Friday and Easter come within twenty-four hours of each other. Pentecost brings both power and persecution. So it goes throughout the Christian year.

We sing "We live in two different worlds". Actually, we live in one world made up of two levels of life that sometimes conflict with one another and sometimes blend in beauty.

The human level alone is shallow and tinny. The divine seems distant from daily demands. One is not better or worse than the other. The blend is what counts.

We give thanks for each. We can count our blessings at the human level, - the beauty and richness of the earth, autumn colours, family life, work to do, bread and roses. Yet even at the most elemental level it is hard to separate one world from the other. Behind the thanksgiving dinner, turkey, cranberries, pumpkin pie and all, is the Giver of gifts. How strange it must be to come to thanksgiving with no one to thank. We rejoice that the earthy and earthly elements of our celebration are signs of love from the Creator. "

We look around the table and bass clef and treble clef come together. These children whom we feed and clothe, in whom we rejoice at thanksgiving, are also God's gift. Kahlil Gibran, the Lebanese mystic poet, reminds us. "They come through you, yet are not from you; and though they are with you, they belong not to you. You are the bow from which your children as arrows are sent forth. Let your bending in the archer's hands be for gladness. For even as he loves the arrow that flies, so he loves also the bow that is stable"

Our love for our partners contains both worlds. It is as down to earth as human passion, but as ethereal as heaven. Good marriages are both gift of God and human acheivement. Pearl Buck wrote, "Love cannot be coaxed or teased. It comes out of heaven unasked and unsought."

The harmony of the two levels, the two worlds, is sometimes hard to achieve. Some families arrive at Thanksgiving this year with homes broken, with a shattering medical report, with a position terminated, with a child in jail, with books revealing a bankruptcy immi-

nent. What shall we then say to these things? We shall say this. Life, at best, is a fragile gift, easily broken. It is perishable and vulnerable, and while it yields the kind of joy that makes Thanksgivings memorable, it may also bring us to this season with no more in our hearts than a cry for help. What shall we say to these things? We shall say that the cry is answered, that nothing shall separate us from the love of God, even our tears.

Prayer
We come to you, O god, our hearts, as always, filled with a strange blend of singing and of sadness. We rejoice in the richness and colour of the season, its mellowness and fruitfulness. In the crowded counters of the marketplace, in the branches heavy with apples, in the bushels of tomatoes ready for sauce, in spicy smelling kitchens, sparkling with jellies and jams, we know your generosity and are grateful. At the same time we bring our prayers for those who come to this time with anxiety, pain, sorrow or confusion. Grant them hope we pray. Amen.

Notes on use of this service, including dates, occasions and possible changes.

Tragedy and the Will of God

Out of the north comes splendour; God is clothed with terrible majesty. He is great in power and justice, and abundant righteousness he will not violate. Therefore we revere him.

Prayer
Our God, we have been bidden to love you with all our hearts and all our minds, yet we have given those hearts to wealth, our minds to the wisdom of this world alone. We have given our strength to personal profit and our hope to earthly gain. Grasp us where we are now and turn us around. Give us a clear vision of the wonder of life in your presence and then the wisdom to choose that way despite all the world's enticements through Christ our Redeemer. Amen.

Scripture Reading
Psalm 23
2nd Corinthians 1:1-7 4:5-12; 16-18

Suggested Hymns
159, 192.

A doctor is called to a home where a lovely little 4 year old lies unconscious. She has been struck by a car. Before the doctor can begin any treatment the girl dies. The minister is already on the scene. The mother is frantic, distraught and screaming.

She cries, "What have we done to deserve this?" This may be simply a cry of despair and a plea for help, yet the implication is there. Tragedy is the result of wrong doing of some sort. A visitation of disaster is a consequence of sin. She might not in a rational moment put it quite so bluntly, but beneath her outcry is a generations-old suspicion that tragedy is God's way of settling debts. The Hewbrew scriptures lean in this direction. One of his would-be comforters tells Job, in the midst of his disasters, "Those who plough iniquity and sow trouble, reap the same." The minister and doctor cannot accept the mother's position.

The minister assures her. "There's no understanding such a thing now, but some day it will make sense. Some day God's purpose will be made clear and then you will understand why she had to be taken now." He might go on to use his favorite illustration of this point - the lovely carpet which, when turned over, displays an ugly tangle of threads and knots, all necessary to create the glorious pattern on the surface.

The doctor objects to this attitude too. Is God, then, a celestial computer operator who is playing a video game with us on the screen. When it suits his purpose he punches our number and, early or late, we disppear from the screen?

The doctor is also a committed Christian. She believes that the life we lead does, and must, contain the possibility of hardship, danger, suffering and tragedy. Without those components we could not grow and mature as children of God. The nature of life on this planet earth is that it contains in it the prospect of tragedy but the amount and degree of tragedy is not directly meted out by God. Life, for many, is harsh, irrational, and unfair. This is the first thing to be said about tragedy. In this life we must forget the notion of "fair" - life is not fair.

The seond thing to say is quite different. No matter what life throws at us, God is in it with us. No matter how dark and diffficult the days are, we are not alone.

> I know not what the future hath
> Of marvel or surprise,
> Assured alone that life and death
> His mercy underlies.

Leslie D. Weatherhead talks of three ways in which we can use the phrase "the will of God." He described the "intentional" will of God, the "circumstantial" will and the "ultimate" will. It would do little good to launch into a discussion of these three with the mother of the little girl at the time of tragedy. If she had been provided with this thought long before the tragedy erupted in her life, she might have been helped in dealing with it.

The intentional will is what God had in mind from the start - life's most perfect unfolding. But because we have wills of our own that often interfere with God's, the circumstantial will of God comes into effect. It is God's will under the circumstances created by our ignorance, rebellion, violence, and sin, as well as by the laws of nature written into creation from the start. It is not God's will that tragedy come, but when it does come, it is God's will that we handle it, with God's help, creatively and triumphantly even in the midst of our tears.

God's ultimate will simply stands for the fact that God will not be permanently

defeated. The love of God will ultimately triumph. The little girl's death was not God's will but one of the circumstances with which God's will must contend as it works its way to its triumphant ending.

No matter what corners us, then, no matter what hurls us down , the Almighty is not using us for target practise. When we are hurt God feels the hurt. Who shall seperate us from the love of God? Nothing. We are more than conquerors through God's love.

Prayer
God, when we stand before stark tragedy we have words. keep us aware, only, of your love, surrounding, enfolding, empowering for the long wait for healing. We ask it in Jesus' name. Amen.

Notes on use of this service, including dates, occasions and possible changes.

21

The Flask

Call
To you,we lift up our eyes, O You who are enthroned in the heavens. Our eyes look to the Lord our God, till he have mercy on us.

Prayer
Maker of all things, loving Parent to all humankind, startle us with your truth and goodness this day, and open our minds and our imaginations to the working of your spirit in us, that we may receive you and one another with joy and fellowship, through Christ our Guide. Amen.

Scripture Reading
Luke 7:36-50

Suggested Hymns
229, 161

Here is one of the most intriguing episodes in the New Testament. If all the rest of the gospels were lost and this preserved we would have the good news - the gospel. It contains the Christian faith in capsule form. Like an opal, the deeper you look into it the more levels and depths are to be seen.

A quick glance and the beauty of it is apparent. Three figures take the stage. Jesus, Simon the Pharisee, and a woman (perhaps Mary Magdalene). The three pair off as the story spins so that we watch Jesus and Simon, Simon and the woman, and Jesus and the woman, and we learn from each encounter - a model of storytelling.

Each of the three characters can be summed up in a symbol. For Simon, a door slammed; for the woman, a flask broken; for Jesus, a hand extended.

Let's look at Jesus and Simon. We find here very different ideas about the nature of the community of faith, the family of God, or, for us, the church.

From the start of his ministry Jesus gathered people into a family. So had the Pharisees. For Jesus, though, the family was inclusive - "Whosoever will - let them come". The Pharisees were exclusive. Simon knew about "This kind of woman" - not one of "our kind". "Do you see this woman?"Jesus said to Simon. Yet Jesus knew that poor Simon could not see the woman. Simon was for family feelings but he was short-sighted about the size of the family tree. He tried to see her but could see only his own labels - she is a sinner, a hippie, a radical, a pinko. I don't know her parents; she's not from around here. She doesn't belong. Simon was a door-slammer.

There is a difference between a church and a club. Some of us belong to private clubs. Such groups have every right to limit membership, to set any standards they wish. But the church is no club. It is God's family on earth, and every human creature is a part of that family by birth. The church is a gathering place for those who acknowledge themselves a part of that family. God made the church to be home for all his children. We who call ourselves "members" are the doorkeepers. Simon was a doorslammer. Jesus was a door opener.

Before we come to Jesus , though, think for a moment about the woman. Once she was through the door what did she do? Once she got into the church how did she act?

She is extravagantly generous., One hears many conjectures about what might be the current values of her flask of ointment. William Barclay tells that women of Israel at that time carried a small vial of costly perfume around their necks in what was called "an alabaster". They were purported to be wedding gifts and worth a great deal, but worth even more from a sentimental value. Whether that were the case or not Jesus was certainly drawn to her by her gracious act. It was so much like what he would do! He valued reckless generosity. The flask, the flask, - the beautifully, extravagant, spontaneous act of self-giving. So like the very God. Robinson Jeffers puts it into poetry.

Is it not by his high superfluousness we know our God? For to equal a need is natural, animal, mineral; But to fling rainbows over the rain, And beauty above the moon, And secret rainbows on the domes of deep seashells, ... That is extravagant kindness.

Now to Jesus. He loved them both. He loves the Simons just as he loves the great givers. The difference is that she was loking for love. Simon was not. The flask broken is the symbol for all time of love outpoured.

Yet the hand of Jesus, extended to lift a "sinner", is a more powerful symbol yet.

She was capable of love. He was the source of love. That hand - reaching - made her love complete. Anne Murray sings of it in "You needed me" with one line "You gave me dignity". May those who come seeking find it in our church.

Prayer
Blessed are you, O God, our Creator, that you have given us life itself, this world in which to live, new life in Christ, and life everlasting in your glory. As we look to our life together in the year that stretches ahead of us, we seek direction from your spirit. Grant us sensitivity to the needs of those around us. May we not look on the world's pain with dry eyes. Grant us wisdom to choose new ways of service, courage to walk in those ways. and the constant challenge of your spirit to reach out to others in loving acceptance, through Christ our Guide, Amen.

Notes on use of this service, including dates, occasions and possible changes.

Saints Alive

Call

Blessed are they who walk not in the counsel of the ungodly, nor stand in the way of sinners, nor sit in the seat of the scornful. But their delight is in the law of the Lord.

Prayer

Our God, visit us in this time of worship we pray. Fill us with the assurance of your love that we may face life confidently. Let your peace grant us serenity and your power fresh strength. Then may we delight in your law, and walk in your ways, through Christ our Lord. Amen.

Scripture Reading

Hebrews 12:1-11

Suggested Hymns

50, 501, if your group is up to it, try 506

If it is possible to have the words printed and an accompanist prepared, try singing "When the Saints Go Marching In".

The New Testament talks a lot about saints. But who, or what, is a saint? A light hearted poet, Bonnie Day, expresses the thoughts some of us entertain about saints.

Angels, devils, saints and sinner,
Look alike to all beginners.
I've discovered much too late
How to differentiate.

How do we differentiate? How can we tell who is a saint?

There are no clear markings. Its questionable whether saints ever wore haloes but, if there are any around now they certainly are not so clearly distinguishable.

There are two quite distinct uses of the word. The church of Rome uses the word in a highly technical manner. Distinguishing saints from ordinary mortals is the task of a highly trained professional who uses precise procedures to determine whether a person qualifies. Morris West tells a gripping story of such a professional in his novel, The Devil's Advocate. If a candidacy is deemed valid then the person joins over twenty thousand others designated saints.

For Paul, and the other New Testament authors, a saint is one who has been baptized into the Christian church. It is unlikely that we would use the term so broadly now.

Somewhere betwen these two meanings lies our accepted use of the word. Poet Laurence Houseman defined a saint as "one who makes goodness attractive". If each of us were to write down the name of someone we have known whom we would call a saint there is probably one characteristic that would mark each of them. ((You might wish to have people take time to write a dname)). All are likely to be giving people. They give time, they give attention, they give love, they give of their substance, they give appreciation, some give their lives. These people are life givers. They stand alongside Jesus Christ who gave all.

They do not so much reflect his glory as allow it to shine through them. As the little girl said after being told that the people in the stained glass windows of her church were saints, "Then saints are people the light shines through".

Probably the prime candidate for sainthood in most peoples' minds would be Mother Theresa of India. She displays all the qualities we have discussed. All of us, however, have encountered our own saints. What of those in the next generation? Where will they find their saints? Most of us would disclaim any prospect of sainthood in ourselves. If every Christian were to disqualify himself, herself, then we would come to the end of sainthood in the church. God knows, literally, have need of saints. The best thing about satinhood is that it is a gift of God to those who would never claim it for themselves. It is a gift that arrives when those for whom it is intended are busy about the Kingdom of God.

Prayer: (The response can easily be memorized, but it would be preferable, if possible, to have the whole prayer printed, with the response indicated)

Lord, we remember your people,
    your saints who have died;
They loved you in life and in death,
    they rest now with you.
Thanks be to God for his saints:
they call us to follow Christ our Lord
Through ages of darkness and sorrow
    they clung to you, Lord;
in prison and danger they found you.
Your will was their peace.
Thanks be to God for his saints:
    they call us to follow Christ our Lord
Rejoicing in you, Lord, they flourished;
    their lives sang your praises.

You gave them bread and your blessing;
    you held them in your love.
Thanks be to God for his saints:
    they call us to follow Christ our Lord
Lord, we remember your people;
    we follow their way.
our praises are joined with their praises.
    Keep us faithful to you.
Thanks be to God for his saints
    they call us to follow Christ our Lord.
Amen.

Notes on use of this service, including dates, occasions and possible changes.

Medals and Models

Call
Lord, you have been our dwelling place in all generations. Before the mountains were brought forth or ever you had formed the earth and the world, from everlasting to everlasting, you are God.

Prayer
O God of all time and space, as our minds range back over time, to the days of our parents and our forebearers, to the ancient stories and even to the edges of time, we are aware of your presence through all and in all. We give you thanks that you are still with us, loving, instructing, directing and empowering. Make us sensitive to the leading of your spirit in our time . Amen.

Scripture Reading
Let us now praise famous men, read in unison from the Hymnary 533
Hebrews 11:32-12:2

Suggested Hymns
253, 133

Let us now praise famous men - and women. The Bible does a great deal of praising famous persons - and some not so famous.The conviction seems to be that in doing so there will be some source of growth and good for ourselves.

One way that Remebrance Day can speak directly to our faith is if those who bear medals can also be our models.

A popular current term is "role model" We become aware of the importance of choosing good role models as we make our choices about a style of life. Remembrance of past battles does bring us accounts of gallantry, valour, committment to national ideals of human rights, and of combatting evil. These strong qualities, evident in armed combat, mark the striking reality of the willingness even to sacrifice life if required.

Still war is seen to be evil and the peaceful settlement of international issues as the only hope of our race, So we hesitate to glorify warfare today.

One expects the Old Testament to glory in bloodshed if it is for the right side. The New Testament uses the language of warfare but recognizes God's love for all his children. We have just listened to stirring words from the Book of Hebrews. Some of the heros who are celebrated in this passage are mighty warriors, but their struggle was often to make God known. They faced incredible odds and took terrifying risks for his sake. Many were famous. Many were not. Note that line in the reading, "Let us now praise famous men...", "And some there be which have no memorial; who are perished as though they had never been." We see those people smiling wistfully in books of remembrance, unsung, but honoured, in general, once a year.

We need both models. The many-medalled ones, with name and fame, but also those more like ourselves. Psychology Today in an article on advertising notes that the use of famous people in ads may be intimidating. A survey found people saying, "I can never be like that" and then resisting whatever was suggested.

Two small boys were sitting on the step in the sunshine examining a new yo-yo. One was reading the small print. "It says this yo-yo is used by champions!". "Well," said the other glumly, "No use us stupid kids trying it then."

While we rightly praise famous men and women, we find, as well, quieter ones who also serve as models. Think back on those who have been models for you. ((You may wish to allow some time for reflection and even, if you wish, for discussion)).

Then comes the day when we realize we are role models for others. How much of what we do is done with awareness that we are watched? Little children appear in parents clothes, mimicing parents walks and ways. At other times gestures, phrases, opinions, reflect those of their parents. The question is, will our own childen, or children we deal with, find their lives enhanced by our presence?

A young sociology student arrived at a church coffee hour lately with a questionnaire for some of her adult friends, which included the sentence stub, "The one thing I would like people to remember about me is...". A very penetrating exercise! It caused a stir at the time and much self-searching afterwards. It carries echoes of familiar words. "This do in remembrance of me." What do we hope others will do in rememberance of us?

Prayer

O Lord, our God, we come to you in a week we have chosen for remembering, - for remembering deeds of courage carried out on behalf of us all, for remembering a great and terrible fear that stalked the earth, for remembering that many still live in fear, but above all, for remembering that you are our God, in good days and bad, in peace and in violence. Let our hearts fill, O God, with thankfulness for the freedom that we enjoy, purchased at great cost. Keep us aware of our responsibility for seeing that others enjoy the same freedom. Purge us of all that makes for strife and war, and may we bring to our daily encounters the same desire for peace and harmony that we wish for those who guide our nations. So may our memories be made holy by your spirit indwelling and directing us in the ways of peace. Amen.

Notes on use of this service, including dates, occasions and possible changes.

Lets Talk Money

Call

Hear the voice of the Psalmist: Behold, O Lord, you desire truth in the inward parts; and in the hidden places you will make us to know wisdom.

Prayer

O God, whose Spirit searches all things and whose love bears all things,we would draw near to you in sincerity, but our untruth often catches us unawares. Saved us from worshipping with our lips while our hearts stand afar off. Save us from the useless labour of trying to conceal our true selves from you who search the hearts of us all, and from whose searching Spirit nothing is hidden. Enable us to lay aside our masks and disguises and to deal with the weakness and selfishness that prevents us from serving either you or our fellows as we would. We pray in the name of Jesus, the true person. Amen.

Scripture Lesson

Luke 19:1-10   Mark 12:41-44

Suggested Hymns

292 (tune 155 a possible alternative) 197

Jesus spoke a great deal about money - and often with the kind of humour contained in the following story.

A prairie farmer appeared at a bank asking for a loan of one dollar!! He acknowledged that it was customary to provide colateral for any loan and produced a ten thousand dollar saving bond. The bond was deposited in the bank vault until the loan was repayed. A year later the farmer reappeared. He renewed the loan, paying the interest on the first year, a nickel and two pennies - seven cents! This happened for several years until finally the bank manager, consumed with curiosity, approached the farmer. "We are quite happy to make this loan but I must ask why you want it. After all, we are holding ten thousand for you. Why would you want to borrow one dollar?" to which the farmer replied, "Do you know how much you folks would charge me per year for a safety deposit box for that bond?"!!

In many of his parables Jesus commended those who showed that kind of brightness and imagination with money.

We have read today two passages out of many stories in which Jesus talked about money. It seems that usually when Jesus got to people's hearts they responded with acts of generosity. The results were in cash, a mite from one (a couple of dollars today), and half a sizeable fortune from the other. It seems that Jesus was convinced that a change of heart was clearly marked by a change in giving.

Martin Luther said that three conversions were necesssary -the head, the heart and the purse.

The scriptures recognize this in the importance attached to idolatry. People are often surprised to find little uneasiness about atheism in the Bible, but a great deal of agitation over idolatry. That might seem strange when one thinks of idols only in terms of wooden or stone statues, but the gods that compete with the one true God are far more subtle and are familiar to us all. How about patriotism, or career, sex or power, - but above all, how about money! Nothing is as likely to challenge God for supreme devotion in our culture. "You cannot serve God and Mammon" does not mean that one cannot have money and serve God, but that one cannot serve money and serve God.

It is a beautiful thing to watch a child enjoying a new toy. One of the joys of parenthood is to provide just the right plaything and see a child totally absorbed in it. But to see an adult equally absorbed in material assets is a deeply disturbing experience.

Archbishop Helda Camera working among the poor of Brazil, seeking justice and fairplay in a jungle of self-seeking, concludes,
> *" I used to think when I was a young priest that Christ had exaggerated when he warned about the dangers of wealth. Today I know better. I know how hard it is to be rich and still possess the milk of human kindness. Money has a dangerous way of putting scales on our eyes, a dangerous way of freezing our hands, eyes, lips and hearts"*

Most of us in North America do not need more things to enjoy, but more time to enjoy what we have. We need even more to find the depth of joy in sharing what we have. When giving yields more pain than pleasure then we are in trouble spiritually.

Dr. Karl Menninger dealing with a wealthy patient asked, "What are you going to do with all your money?" The patient answered, "Just worry about it, I suppose." Menninger pursued the matter, "Do you get pleasure out of worrying?" "No", the man replied, "But its better than the terror I feel when I think of giving it away." Menninger's conclusion was interesting. "Difficulty in giving is a symptom of illness. Generous people are rarely emotionally ill."
In his own language Menninger is repeating Jesus' teaching.

Prayer
We come to worship, O God, aware that we are gifted. You have provided for our every need; good food, shelter, knowledge, skill, friendship, affection. In our ignorance we often feel that these are our own posessions by right. In our best moments we know that they are your gifts and behind all life's wonders we find your very presence, Creator, Giver. For all of this we thank you. May we spend ourselves and our substance in striving for Christ's goals May we hunger and thirst after righteousness, and may we be the merciful and the peacemakers in the midst of injustice and strife. So would we give of our time and our talent, our treasure and our toil in the name of Jesus. Amen.

Notes on use of this service, including dates, occasions and possible changes.

In Praise of Puritans

Call

Your word is a lamp to our feet and a light on our path. Your testimonies are wonderful. We would keep them in our souls.

Prayer

Eternal God, through the centuries you have watched over your people and guided those who were open to your leading. We thank you for the illustrious company of those who have kept themselves true to your ways and have left an heritage of obedience and trust. May we, in our own time, and in our own ways, be as faithful. May our confidence be rewarded by the assurance of your presence with us now as we worship, as we learn and grow, and as we leave this place to serve you in the lives of those we meet.

Scripture Reading

Matthew 5:1-7, 28.

Suggested Hymns

361, 58

Almost 400 years ago, in this month, a sailing ship anchored off what is now called Rhode Island. The ship was the Mayflower. It carried a small group of religious outcasts from Europe. They built the first permanent English speaking community in North America. This month the U.S. Thanksgiving celebrates their courage, determination, and faithfulness.

No immigrants to North America have ever been more carefully screened for purity, piety, good character, and proper theology. These were the "pilgrims", the puritans who were to write the beginnings of North American lifestyle in indelible ink.

For them the Bible was the foundation of all thought and action. It provided them with a total pattern for emotional, intellectual, social and civil life. The puritans wanted a "purer" form of religion than they had experienced in Europe. They wanted to cleanse the church of hierarchy, of set prayers, of vestments, of outward signs, of all that might detract from purity of thought and worship - including even wedding rings and Christmas!! Added to this, they had a powerful sense of destiny and purpose. Cotton Mather, a fiery orator of the early settlement, spoke of them as the "chosen people, covenanted to God, to go out and settle the new land for Him". The pulpit had a large place in their lives. The preacher was also teacher, journalist, community organizer, and political commentator. One writer says, "Instead of staying home and reading the paper, the Puritans made history six days of the week and on the seventh came to the meeting house to hear the preacher explain it to them."

Puritans are easily criticized, yet we could benefit from an injection of some of their better qualities today.

They bequeathed us a cluster of ideas that are hard to analyuze precisely but they include these four.

1. *Industry.* The Puritans lived by the

conviction that God was glorified in hard work and the attendant results. We call it the Protestant work ethic" today. Work for them was more than doing a job. It was the way in which God called out a persons's entire range of capacities and talents.

2. *Morality.* They leaned heavily on the "thou shalt nots" and included within those more than we would (light music, dancing, fine clothes and thatre) yet they felt that they were only sacrificing some small pleasures for a deeper dimension of joy. Many would agree that we have moved too far in the opposite direction to the point where we will restrict ourselves in no way.

A speaker at a major international meeting said, "I find that I must use the word 'sin' without prefacing it with 'so-called...sin' and without joking about it." Was this a clergyperson speaking? Hardly! It was the Presidential address of O. Hobart Mowrer, to the American Psychiatric Association. On the thunderstones of Moses' stone tablets the foundation of our western culture was laid. We are unlikely to strengthen the structure by pulling out the foundation.

3. *Simplicity.* The early puritans were forced to lead simple lives. Their descendants chose to. For many years each Sunday the whole community would gather at the seashore to look out over the Atlantic in stillness. Then they would silently make their way to church. A consistency of purpose must have grown out of such practises.

4. *Community.* There are many books on the market prompting us, and instructing us to look out for No., 1. The puritan may have at times been too in-volved in the life of his neighbour, yet her motives were genuine concern for the welfare of the community and of the neighbour. Again, we have much to learn.

Prayer
We confess, O God, that we have looked within for guidance rather than out to your word. Where our own lives have not humbled us enough to make us attentive to your word, then hold before us the wonder of the pure life of your son that we may wish as full and rich a lives for ourselves and so learn to obey. We bring to you, O God, our concern for all in need, close by and far off. We pray for all those in our midst worried, in pain, fearful or doubtful. We pray for our own nation torn by division and disagreement. We pray for a world of nations in distress, and in our helplessness, pray that your own wisdom may prevail in the counsels of nations, through Christ our Lord. Amen.

Notes on use of this service, including dates, occasions and possible changes.

31

Children of Light

Call

Jesus said, "I am the light of the world".
Another time he said to his followers
"You are the light of the world".

> Whenever I come on kelp-stained
> nets
> Drying along the sands,
> I think of four bronzed fishermen,
> And my heart understands
> How joyfully they laid aside
> Their nets by Galilee,
> To follow one clear beacon light
> Across eternity.

Scripture Reading
Isaiah 60:1-5; 19,20   John 12:27-36

Suggested Hymns
274,   364 (alternative tune 294)

Modern Israel has some striking archi-
tecture. One of the most impressive
buildings is the Shrine of the Book. Built
to house the Dead Sea scrolls, it has a
brilliant white dome top shaped like the
lid of the jars in which the scrolls were
discovered. One must stoop to enter as
through a cave. The whole of the building is subterranean. The entraceway is
guarded by a high basalt wall - pitch
black, in obvious contrast to the dome.
Here is black and white - light and darkness - a reminder of the Essene community that copied the scrolls and hid them.
They called themselves the children of
light, and all others the children of darkness. It is an unusual term in Jewish
thought and Jesus' use of it seems to link
him with that community.

Jesus used the term during the last week
of his life. He had experienced the
anointing in Bethany, and the triumphal
entry into Jerusalem on Palm Sunday.
He was reflecting on it when Phillip and
Andrew brought a group of Greek no-
tables to meet him. Jesus said to them
all, "The light is with you a little longer.
Walk while you have the light, lest the
darkness overcome you. ... While you
have the light, believe in the light, that
you may become sons of light."

John takes the symbol of light right back
to the beginning of the story. When it
came time for him to write it all down he
saw the opening chapter of Jesus' life
bathed in light.

We could spend time cataloguing all the
meanings of this one symbol, but they
are all caught up in the words of the
Psalmist. "My soul longs for thee more
than they that watch for the morning."
Here are the deepest yearnings - dawn
yearnings, Advent yearnings - in the
watch that ends the night. A new day is
dawning. Those who have seen *Cats*
will know what powerful feelings are
evoked by the words and music of
Memory:

> Daylight, I must wait for the sunrise.
> I must think of the new life. And I
> mustn't give in. When the dawn
> comes, tonight will be memory too,
> and a new day will begin.

Walk in the light of God's hope."Yea
though I walk through the valley of the
shadow of death I shall fear no evil."
Some have encountered the saints of
God whose faces actually light up in

prayer, made radiant by the inner glow of God's sure presence.

If we walk in the light we too may grow luminous for others.

An old favorite camp song carried the notion of light. "This little light of mine" but it may have overemphasized the "small corner". The Essenes kept their light to their own small corner. We are called to bring light to the world.

Jesus second use of the term helps carry the idea further. It is found in a strange place - in that remarkable Parable of the Unjust Steward. The man, about to be fired for embezzling, gets in good with some of his master's clients by discounting their debts, neatly feathering his own nest at his employer's expense. The astonishing thing is that Jesus appeared to commend the man for his shrewdness, saying, "So the children of this world are wiser in their time than the children of light."

The fact is clear that Jesus did admire sharp people. The parables are full of them, though this is the most dramatic example. He seems to be saying, "If only you would take being children of light as seriously - with the same realism, the same forethought and originality, with the same determination and application. What a disciple band we would have!"

We may get the message if we compare the energy, cash, reading, training, that we give to golf, curling, sailing, or whatever may be oour favorite recreation, with what we give to adult faith and action. An old-time New England preacher talking to his congregation about this parable said, "The steward chose his path like a fool and walked in it like a wise person. We choose our path like a wise person but walk in it like a fool." Jesus would likely agree.

In Advent, while we think about the stable and the Babe, it is well to keep in mind that the child became the man who left us with this strong expectation.

Prayer
We look toward the light of the Bethlehem stable, O God, and pray that you will come like the morning, scattering our darkness and doubt. Break through our darkness, whatever its source may be, to grant us the hope and assurance that belongs to this season. Amen.

Notes on use of this service, including dates, occasions and possible changes.

Leading Lady

Call
Search us, O God, and know our hearts;
try us and see if there be any wicked way
in us, and lead us in the way everlasting.

Prayer
With grateful hearts, O God, and with
joyous spirits, we prepare to celebrate
the coming of your son. We praise and
thank you that in him we discover love,
complete and whole. We pray for understanding of such love, and for determination to let love rule in our hearts, now
and always, Amen.

Scripture Reading
Isaiah 62:1-12   Luke 1:26-38 (followed
by unison reading of the Magnificat,
Hymnary 525

Suggested Hymns
57, 72

Every drama has its leading lady. The
Christmas drama is no exception.
Clearly it is Mary, the mother. Dorothy
Sayers, English author, in her Christmas
play, *The Man Born to Be King*, has
Mary speak to the Wise Men, "I feel as
though I were holding the whole world
in my arms - the sky, and the sea, and the
green earth, and all the seraphim. And
then again everything becomes simple
and familiar and all I know is that he is
just my dear son." Mary is, in fact, the
leading lady for the whole Christian
drama. Quiet and humble, it is hard to
imagine her the center of so much con-
troversy. A great amount of ink, and
much blood, has been spilt in debating
her place in Christian devotion, but
none can deny the respect given her by
the biblical writers, especially Luke.
What do we find in the figure of Mary
for ourselves?

When Sayers play was first produced on
BBC it caused a near-riot because she
had cast her players with various British
accents. Her stage directions include
fascinating character sketches of the
roles. Of Mary, she writes, "She must be
played with dignity and sincerity, and
with perfect simplicity. Her voice is
sweet, but not sugary; and there must be
no trace of any kind of affectation. A
very slight touch of an accent - perhaps
a faint shadow of Irish quality, would be
of assistance."

What we find in Mary, above all, it
seems, is a supreme example of recep-
tivity. Mary is the model of openess to
the will of God at work. There is expec-
tancy and willingness. She seems waiting on bended knee for God to act. The
Advent spirit is embodied in her humble
confidence.

Follow the sequence of her encounter
with Gabriel to see the ideal reception of
a word from God. At the start she is
disturbed. The presence of God comes
often as a disturbing and disruptive
experience.

Then she is perplexed. How can this be?
Often when God's will is made known
to us, it shifts us off course. We are
puzzled by the direction in which our
lives are being pushed. Scripture often
puzzles us with riddle-like sayings.

Perplexity leads to awe and wonder before the mystery of God's dealings.

Her third response is obedience. "Whatever it is, I am ready". Mary's is a simple story with a complex relationship with God underlying it all. Mary's response to God is what makes her "blessed". "Blessed are you among women".

If Mary is blessed then blessing has little to do with outward success. To have your baby hundreds of miles from home, amongst strangers, in a cow barn, and to flee from the wrath of a powerful tryrant. Then to return to an obscure village, to be widowed as a young mother with a family to raise. Some blessing!! Some favour!!

Blessing, it seems, is to be found in working within the will of God and knowing that you do so. Listen once more to Mary in the Dorothy Sayers' play. "You see,,, when the angel's message came to me the Lord put a song in my heart. I suddenly saw that wealth and cleverness were nothing to God. No one is too unimportant to be his friend. ... I am humbly born, yet the power of God came upon me; I am very foolish and unlearned yet the Word of God was spoken to me; and I was in deep distress when my baby was born yet he filled my life with love. So I know very well that wisdom and power and sorrow can live together with love; for me, the child in my arms is the answer to all the riddles."

And so Mary, as she takes her place as leading lady, becomes, herself, a part of the answer to life's riddles.

Prayer
Blessed are you, O God, our Maker, that you have given us the miracle of Bethle-

hem, a sign of peace and a promise of love.

Blessed are you who have given us in Mary, the mother, a model of motherhood, a model of faith. May we learn from her the qualities of true humility, openess, awe and obedience that made her blessed. Our God, may this sacred season bring us close to the realities of the first Christmas. My we feel the lonliness that many experience at Christmas, bereavements that stir hurting memories for many in our own midst, the emptiness known to travellers who spend the season for from home, the uneasiness that many feel wondering what the season can mean for them. We would not hide from these feelings behind the festivity of our celebrating. While we rejoice in our life together, keep us sensitive to all for whom this is a painful time. We ask it in Jesus name. Amen.

Notes on use of this service, including dates, occasions and possible changes.

Christ the Way

Call

Blessed are the undefiled in the way, who walk in the way of the Lord. Blessed are they that keep his testimonies and that seek him with the whole heart.

Prayer

O Lord, we turn our faces like the wise Men of old, toward the star of Bethlehem. As we begin our journey to the manger we know how much easier it will be to watch commercials than to keep the Christmas comet in view. Mad haste will keep us from looking up, the jangling noise of the cash register will distract us, the shopping mall will deflect our best intentions so that we may arrive at Christmas Eve without wonder or joy. Keep us on our pilgrimage, O God, and bring us to that wondrous evening with heart and mind on tip-toe, that we may rejoice with the heavens and welcome the babe into our own hearts. It is in his name that we ask it. Amen.

Scripture Reading

Isaiah 40:1-5; 9-11   Luke 1:39-56

Suggested Hymns

428,   421
You may wish to include a lighting of Advent candles.

G.K. Chesterton has provided some of our most memorable words about Christmas. In a short epigram he sums up its meaning:

Christmas is good news,

But if you ask me what it is, I know not.
It is a track of feet in the snow.
It is a lantern showing a way.
It is a door set open.

This is a fine contrast to some of the soupy, sentimental words we hear at Chrstmas. Lean and tough - like Christmas. that first Christmas, at any rate.

The first name for the new fellowship that was later called the church was "followers of the Way". Today Christians speak of the faith journey. Christianity is not a room but a road, not a resting place but a route march, not a conclusion but a quest. It is more than a theory about life in this universe, more than a superb set of rules written on paper - it is a path along which we journey, it is a way of life.

This idea has appeal for North Americans who have, as a nation, always been a people on the move, on the road. Think of some of the feats of pioneering courage that belong to your own families. It took astounding nerve to cross the Atlantic in the tiny *Mayflower* or on the vessels that carried settlers up the St. Lawrence. The same steel nerves were needed on the river routes that carried explorers further and further inland, and then finally over the unbelievable rockies and out to the coast to meet other daring travellers who had sailed up the coast.

The nerve must have come to them "on the way". Intimidated by risks known and unknown, still they pushed on trusting that they would learn to cope, on the way.

The Bible is full of that spirit. Abraham and Sarah went out not knowing where they would end. Moses and his flock followed a pillar of cloud by day and fire by night across the wilderness. The Wise Men journeyed following a star. T.S. Eliot has them say, "A cold coming we had of it. Just the worst time of year for a journey, and such a journey. The way was deep and the weather sharp. The very dead of winter."

Though we may not literally make the kind of journeys these people did, movement is expected of us - movement of the spirit. One of the desert fathers of the 4th Century, St. Sarapion of Egypt, made a pilgrimage to Rome, a long and risky journey then. He was fascinated to hear of a saintly woman living a life of prayer and devotion, but never leaving her room. Skeptical about her way of life, for he felt travel was the best way to learn, he called on her. He was abrupt. "Why are you sitting here?" She replied, "I am not sitting, I am on a journey". Spiritually we can always be on the move. We journey through the inward space of our hearts and our spirits.

At the core of the Christian life is walking with Jesus, feeling the lift of his spirit meeting with ours, along the way. In a film that won her an Oscar just before her death Geraldine Page provides a parable of "the way". In *Trip to Bountiful* she plays an old woman, Carrie Watts, who wants above all to return once more to her childhood home before she dies. The home town was Bountiful, Texas. She had buried two babies there, was young and lovely

there, and had been wanted there. It is a great story of a trek, like the westward wagon tales. She travels on bus, with wiles, tears, cunning and some deviousness, singing hymns and psalms all the way. The town is gone. Her old home is decaying. But she made it for a moment, and that was all that mattered. She sits in the ruins and cries, and so do we all. We all cry, knowing that no home is the same the day after tomorrow. We know the importance of renewing contacts, but we know that nothing can remain the same., We travel on. This month we will all make it home, home for Christmas. We are travelling to Bethlehem where all men - all women - are at home. Bethlehem is our Bountiful. Chesterton writes in another poem: *To an open house in the evening/Home shall all folk come,/To an older place than Eden/ And a taller town than Rome./To the end of the way of the wandering star,/To the things that cannot be and are./To the place where God was homeless,/ And all men are at home"*.

Notes on use of this service, including dates, occasions and possible changes.

In the Flesh

Call

Arise, shine, for your light has come, and the glory of the Lord has come upon you.

Prayer

Lord God of the star and the stable, of the dark night and the lonely birth, of the angel song and the shepherd's awe, Christmas comes with such a mystic mix of emotion that we need you to steady us, and focus our thoughts. Many of us have left behind gifts still to wrap, food to prepare, notes to write, friends to call. Quiet us now, as we step out of the stream of life for a moment, and give us as fresh vision of what this season is about. May song and scripture, and meditation carry us closer to the heart of Christmas, for the sake of the blessed babe, even Jesus. Amen.

Scripture Reading

Arise, shine - read in unison. Hymnary 524   Luke 2:22-35

Suggested Hymns

64,   427

At a time when many Roman Catholic churches were simplifying their decor in Quebec some strange things happened to some of the "terminated" statues. For a while on Highway ll, north of St. Jerome, at a curve in the highway where a junkyard was located, a monstrous statue of Jesus had been deposited against a wire fence beside the highway. The figure towered over the highway, arms outstretched in a gesture that seemed to bless the passing motorists and their autos. Twisted auto bodies surrounded it, a patates frîtes   stand stood at its base, tattered election posters obscured parts of the looming figure, and gas fumes permeated all. Still the gentle Saviour stood, arms extended in gracious benediction. It was all so wrong - and all so right!

The word became flesh and dwelt among us. Jesus is as timely as a space lab or kilobytes in a megadisc. If God had chosen to wait a while, Jesus could have walked onto the terrace of the apartment across from the highway, or into the junkyard office, or up to the french fry stand. He is as timeless as the eternal strength of the stone from which the statue was hewn.

The word became flesh - in one time and one place, yet "In the beginning was the word", and at the end of time there shall be the word. He is dateless, yet always current.

This is one of the deeper meanings of Christmas. Underlying all the gift wrap and office parties, Salvation Army kettles and hokey commercials with Santa guzzling Coke, Bob Hope's visit to a military hospital, or Grandmas' arrival from Pincher Creek, is the assurance that Jesus was and is and is to come. The word is still made flesh.

At Christmas we find God in a stable, smelly beasts, an awkward childbirth and all, and realize that there is no telling where he will next appear. Sydney Carter has us sing, *"Who can tell what other* *cradle,/high above the milky way,/still may rock the King of heaven/ on another Christmas day?"*There is no telling what other visits he has in mind, what other ambushes he has laid. We are never safe from God's arrivals. That is a serious part of the Christmas message.

And he is never safe from us. He has made himself vulnerable That is the Good Friday message. Even that message is anticipated in the dark side of Christmas, the lurking soldiers of Herod, the flight westward into Africa.

The late news these nights seems so out of sync with our Christmas preparations, or is it the other way around? The scenes from all around the world are a far cry from the angel anthem of peace on earth. Even our lust for power and callous efficiency are haunted by the Christmas celebration. That baby whose birth we await disturbs all our competition and rivalry, all our complaining and cheating, all our fighting and hating. No longer can we hate without feeling his judgement. His love is stronger than our selfishness. When Christmas clashes with the late news we come away awed by the conviction that Christmas is the more real. "I have come that you might have life - and that more abundantly." Welcome to life this Christmas!

Prayer

Great God, you who are beyond our sight, above our thought, infinite, eternal, and unsearchable. Your wisdom shines in all your works. Your glory is shown in your goodness to us all. Your grace and truth are revealed in the blessed child of Bethlehem. We thank you now for the magic of Christmas, this special season of gladness and joy. We celebrate the song of peace sung by the angels, spoken by your Christ, passed on by your church from age to age. We celebrate your gift of love in our families, in neighbourhood parties, among good friends, in the festive spirit on the streets and in the shops. We would sing your praise for you have visited us with your goodness.

We recall that at your first coming you dwelt with lowly animals and with humble folk. So we pray for all whose hearts are heavy because they cannot provide the gifts they would, all who come to this season dreading the first sight of an empty place at the Christmas table, all whom your love has left as yet unchanged, the criminal, the derelict, the addict, the proud, the arrogant. Bless each one we pray, and may the spirit of Christmas bring some light to all who sit in darkness. Amen.

Notes on use of this service, including dates, occasions and possible changes.

The Uses of Interruption

Call

The hour comes and now is when the true worshippers shall worship the Lord in spirit and in truth; for the Lord seeks such to worship him.

Prayer

Lord, you have been our dwelling place in all generations. Before the mountains were brought forth or ever you had formed the earth and the world, even from everlasting to everlasting, you are God. We give you thanks for the assurance and confidence that this knowledge brings to our lives, calming and directing us as no other truth can do. Amen

Scripture Reading

Mark 5:21-34   6:30-34

Suggested Hymns

49,   249.

It is easy when reading scripture to overlook the human touches in anticipating the divine. Think of the story we have just heard. The disciples are back from their first field trip, their first attempt to minister on their own. They are exhausted. They have a stories to tell, questions to ask.

Jesus, sensitive to their need, suggests, "Come with me by yourselves to a quiet place and we will rest awhile." They cross the lake by boat, but on the opposite shore the disciples are dismayed. The crowds have followed them! Now hear this sentence!. "When they came to shore Jesus saw the great crowd and his heart......." In your own mind, now, complete the sentence.

His heart fell.. His heart was weary . No!! "His heart went out to them." Once more his plans were disappointed, his schedule thrown off. He had planned a quiet retreat and ended up with a mass rally. Before the day is over he had fed 5,000!

A series of interruptions had begun some time back when he had been teaching and was interrupted by Jarius pleading for his daughter's life. Then on the way to the healing Jesus was interrupted again by a woman asking for healing. It is impressive to watch Jesus handle interruption. Think of frustrating interruptions that you've experienced recently. They do dreadful things to blood pressure and tension level. Mark, by linking these stories, is offering us a lesson in Christian grace. A gracious handling of interruption indicates maturity.

More than that, we may detect in Jesus' response to interruption a significant clue to his understanding of how God makes his will known. There is a deep theological thread here. We believe that God has a will for each of us - daily. This being true, may not interruption be one the methods of making his will known?

Christians sail under sealed orders. We find God's will as we are "on the way", doing it. Mark's description of Jesus' day represents an efficiency expert's nightmare. From a point of view of a time study, it was a disaster. From a devotional viewpoint it was a day of glory. Detours often have more to give us than the main road. It is when we discover that God's agenda may differ from ours and learn to treat interruption with a sense of adventure that we find ourselves walking in Jesus' way.

On the other hand God does use schedules as well as interruptions, and Christian maturity requires that we make the difficult choices between them.

An even harder assignment for the Christian is to see that some of life's painful interruptions can provide God with opportunities to break through to us. This sort of Interruption does more than disrupt a day, it disrupts a life. There is infinite sadness in the words "My name wasn't there." - not on the honour roll, not on the promotions posting, not on the team , not in the headlines the day after the election. I have not simply been interrupted; I have been shot down.

Are we to believe, then, that it is God's will that a young girl finds after a summer of daily practice that she has not after all been accepted for the National Ballet School? Is it enough to say that whenever God closes one door he opens another?

What we can say is that when those circumstances block God's will or ours he does supply an alternative. Sydney Carter has written a book of poems titled "Nothing Fixed or Final" . It is a good summary of the way God works.
Disappointment then becomes not an anchor but wind in the sails. Few public figures suffered the amount of interruption and disappointment that Adlai Stevenson did, but he often quoted the well known passage that contains, "I asked God for strength that I might acheive,: I was made weak that I might humbly obey. ... I asked for all things, that I might enjoy life; I was given life that I might enjoy all things."

To say that all things work for good is to say that within the tragedy and tears, the shattered plans and rebuilt lives, in unfair trials and in crosses on hilltops, God strives for us, beside us, through us, to reweave disappointments and interruptions into garments of glory.

Prayer
O God, Creator of time and space, Sustainer of all life, we thank you for blood and breathe, for love and laughter, for human hearts and holding hands. We thank you that you have given us a model of your expectations in Jesus. We pray that we may follow his example in using interruption to your glory. Amen.

Notes on use of this service, including dates, occasions and possible changes.

Good, good time

The steadfast love of the Lord is from everlasting to everlasting upon those who revere him, and his righteousness to children's children.

Prayer
Eternal God, in whose sight a thousand years are as an evening past; as you have led us in days gone by, so guide us now as we enter this new year. We confess that in the year past we have lived too often for ourselves, ignoring the needs of those around us,and ignoring the pain of the world. We haved passed by on the road the hungry, the oppressed, the poor. We have hidden from the probing and the seeking of your prompting Spirit.Forgive us, we pray, and free us to live in liberty with you. In Jesus' name. Amen.

Scripture Reading
Psalm 90
2 Corinthians 5:l6-6:2

Suggested Hymns
388, 377 (Alternate Tune suggested 28)

No topic is more common at New Years than "time". Think of all we do with time - we gain time, fight time, lose time, find time, beat time, kill time, waste time, save time... and so on, and on. There is no end to the quotes one can accumulate regarding time. One that conveys much is on an old clock in Chester Cathedral.
   When as a child I laughed and wept, time crept.
   When as a boy I dreamed and talked, time walked.

When I became a full grown man, time ran.
Then later, as I older grew, time flew.
Soon I shall find, while travelling on, time gone.

We are all deeply aware of time and its passage. Some want to slow it down. "Time, you old gypsy man, will you not stay."

Other rush it. "What a drag. I can hardly wait".Time is the only resource that each of us is proud to admit we lack.

"Time management" is a favorite topic for after dinner speakers in the business world. The fact is, there is no such thing. There is only management of ourselves with regard to time. Despite difficulty with the term, as this new year begins, we will take a a look at time managment for the Christian.

The starting point must be the recognition that time is a gift of God, to be used with appreciation and respect. Paul wrote to the Collosians, "Make the best possible use of your time".That is the clear message of our Puritan ancestors. They were distressed by time wasted because one's devotion was proven by one's production. In turn, this conviction generated the "Protestant work ethic".

Uneasiness about the Protestant work ethic stems from the fact that its practitioners have often been more work-centered than God-centered. There are worse errors. Calvin, one of its founders, wrote of the work ethic, "There is no task so sordid or base that, provided you obey your calling in it, it will not shine and be reckoned precious in God's sight"

Most jobs can be enjoyable. Alan McPhee well-known to CBC listeners in Canada, said in an interview, "My motto is, 'far better to be a radio announcer than work for a living'." He followed up with, "Just watch me in the corridors grinning from ear to ear!". Listeners to "Eclectic Circus" can feel the grin. Making work an act of joy is probably the first lesson to be learned about Christian time management.

In a New Year's interview regarding future trends most of the participants mentioned issues of peace, poverty and so on. Noted commentator, Eric Sevaried's "issue" was leisure. How does "loafing" fit into our notion of Christian stewardship? The Bible links it to the nature of God as surely as it does work. On the 7th Day God rested.

We have thought of work time and leisure time. Family time also deserves attention. Time spent in family games, camping, travel, provides rare opportunities to listen, to care and to show concern. Finding words to help another express her feelings; time spent in shared laughter or shared tears - all these are growing ground for family life, but each requires a committment of time.

In the words of the old hymn, "Take time to be holy". Public worship, private devotion, hours of study, time for prayer - we sometimes fail to get these onto our agendas.

Skill in budgeting can be applied to time

as well as to cash. Each is a limited commodity. Each requires thought and planning. "So teach us to number our days that we may apply our hearts to wisdom." says the Psalmist.

Prayer
Maker of all time and space, God who was before time or place, we thank you for the gift of years. We are grateful for all that gives our lives shape and design, for the dependable round of days, the annual cycle of seasons, and the seasons of the heart. We thank you, too, for fresh beginnings, and pray that in the use of these your gifts we may find closeness with your timeless spirit, through Christ our Lord. Amen.

Notes on use of this service, including dates, occasions and possible changes.

What's an Epiphany?

We have heard a rather lengthy portion of Paul's letter to the church in Ephesus. He brings it to a climax with these words.

"That you being rooted and grounded in love, may have the power to comprehend with all the saints, what is the breadth and length and height and depth, and to know the love of Christ which surpasses all knowledge, that you may be filled with the fullness of God."

""That you may be filled with the fullness of God". That is quite an order!

The fullness comes in small units. Those small units might be called "epiphanies".

With Christmas passed we come to the celebration of epiphany. But what is an epiphany? You might ask as a multiple choice question:
•is it a light French pastry?
•something ministers wear on high holy days?
•an ancient woodwind instrument?
•a lovely scarlet flower found in the Adirondaks?
•or none of the above?

None of the above is correct. The church calendar marks January Sixth as "epiphany" - the day that marks the coming of the wise men. It also marks the going of the wise men as they returned home carrying the news of Jesus to the rest of the world.

What does the word mean? What is an epiphany?

One answer came in a recent *Saturday Review* article. It dealt with the newest developments in photography. It told of the Cambridge Laboratory of the Polaroid Company's newest product. The SX-70 - an instant colour camera that focusses by sonar. They call it "the ultimate painless epiphany machine"!

Here is a clue - a flash of beauty recorded. An epiphany.

Students of English literature will know that the word epiphany was used by James Joyce. In one of his novels his leading character, Stephen Hero, overhears a conversation on the streets of Dublin. He recalls, "It was a triviality, really, but somehow it threw a sudden light across my appreciation for other people". Hero decides to make a collection of such moments in a "book of epiphanies". In another novel a young man describes an epiphany as a "sudden spiritual manifestation - the most delicate and evanescent focussing moment".

An epiphany, then, is a moment which rescues from the commonplace the radiance of an experience,"the enchantment of the heart". We, too, have known those miraculous moments when a phrase, a gesture, a scene, a word, has startled us with wonder, and we have come away refreshed and renewed.

The wise men kneeling at the manger is the perfect picture of such a moment.

This is the reality of God breaking into our world of things and patterned behaviour to capture our hearts by surprise for a moment. One glimpse and God is gone, but we are never again the same persons.

Out of darkness, into the light of the stable; a moment of wonder, and then into the darkness again. But the moment of wonder goes with us. Such is epiphany.

As we enter the new year we could make our own "book of epiphanies". We will want not so much a scrapbook, as a photo album. Like polaroid's epiphany machine we open ourselves to the moment, "click", and its on record, an epiphany! No one epiphany tells the whole story. Even the wise men knew only a part of the story when they left the stable, but they had had an epiphany. Light had broken in on their darkness and they would never be the same again.

Annie Dillard describes September in Tinker Creek. Migrating redwing blackbirds were making a great racket. When she went to investigate a hundred birds materialized from one tree. She writes, "I saw a tree, then a rush of colour, then a tree again. It was as if the leaves of the tree had been freed from a spell in the form of red-wing blackbirds." For her, an epiphany of the wonder of God's creation.

It is out of a number of such epiphanies that we shall build our lives into the pattern of Paul's letter to Ephesus, "the comprehension of what is the breadth and length and depth and height of God's love." So that we may be filled - gradually, bit by bit, - with the fullness of God.

Prayer
We pray for a "change of heart", O God, so our eyes may open, so our hearts may beat, so our voices may sing. May the wonder of your presence all around us now fill us with joy. Amen.

Notes on use of this service, including dates, occasions and possible changes.

Jonah and Ecumenism

Call

Behold how good and pleasant it is when brothers and sisters dwell together in harmony.

Prayer of Confession

The group's response, *Reconcile us, O Christ, by your cross*, can be quickly memorized, though it is smoother if it can be printed for the participants, either the one line response, or the whole prayer.)

Across the barriers that divide race from race
Reconcile us, O Christ by your cross.

Across the barriers that divide rich from poor
Reconcile us, O Christ by your cross.

Across the barriers that divide people of different faiths
Reconcile us, O Christ by your cross.

Across the barriers that divide Christians
Reconcile us, O Christ by your cross.

Across the barriers that divide men and women, young and old.
Reconcile us, O Christ, by your cross.
Amen.

Leader: Sisters and brothers, I proclaim to you that God is love. In that love our sins are forgiven and our fears are banished;
So know that the love of God is for us.
Amen.

Scripture Lesson

Jonah 3:1-5, v. 10; 4:1-11
Matthew 5:43-48

Suggested Hymns

148, 149 *Try to locate Walter Farquarson's excellent "Though ancient walls may still stand proud..."*

Jonah has a good deal to tell us in the Week of Prayer for Christian Unity. There are probably more funny stories and cartoons about Jonah than about any Biblical figure other than Noah, yet for our time this book is a powerfully significant document.

The book of Jonah arose out of an historical crisis in the life of ancient Israel. 600 years before the birth of Jesus the eastern seaboard of the Mediterranean was overun by the armies of the Babylonian empire. Jerusalem was destroyed and the temple sacked. Many citizens were taken captive and spent years in exile in Babylon.

When at last the Babylonian empire tumbled before the might of Persia (roughly foreshadowing the current conflict between Iran and Iraq) the captives were allowed to return to Israel. Their mood was one of high anger. They had retained their racial purity in Babylon and they were determined to do so back home. They dreamt of the wrath of God destroying all the surrounding nations that had troubled them so sorely. Their northern neighbours aroused their anger especially and Nineveh in Assyria was a major city in that territory.

During the period of captivity many immigrants had infiltrated Israel, searching for secure settlement and fertile land. The Jews who had been left behind had accomodated them. The returning exiles wanted an exclusive Jewish society, but many of the long-standing citizens disagreed. Out of the tension between the points of view came two pieces of literature well known to us all, Ruth and Jonah. Jonah was a scathing satire, a clever short story that might today be submitted to Esquire magazine. It ridiculed the hard-line party, but went even further in pointing out how the conservative attitude actually betrayed the faith of the founders of Israel.

The story is familiar. Jonah was a great preacher. At one point God touched his life and directed him to the sprawling and decadent city of Nineveh. He was to mount an evangelistic crusade there that would save the people from the wrath of God. Jonah had no wish to spare the people of Nineveh. Nothing pleased him more than the prospect of their violent destruction. So rather than try to avert God's anger from Nineveh Jonah ran away, expecting that if he could get out to sea he would be beyond God's reach. The spirit of God, however, followed him in the form of a storm. To Jonah's credit he did take responsibility for the life-threatening storm and allowed himself to be thrown overboard. Swallowed by a large fish, he lived three days in its innards, then was deposited on the shore. So far, the story is well known. The remaining portion tells how Jonah's preaching in Nineveh was successful despite his inner desire for failure. The people repented and God spared the city. Jonah, for his part, was furious and he stomped petulantly out of the final scene. Many who heard the story must have recognized themselves at this point. They had lost the whole purpose of being God's chosen people - chosen to reveal God's love to the world. They had mistaken the call to service for the call to privilege.

The church is in danger of doing the same thing. The reason for Israel's existence - and the church's - is to be a channel of God's love to all the world - to the oikos mene - the household of God (from which we get our word ecumencial). The Week of Prayer for Christian Unity can be a time in which we ask what the church is doing to make clear the unity - the familyhood - of all people. An understanding of our mission to the whole household of God influences the way we think about peace and justice, but also about immigration and people of other faiths and races. May we not fall into Jonah's bitter plight!

Prayer
Confront us, O God, with all the hidden prejudices and fears that deny and betray our prayers. Remove from us all false sense of supriority and teach us how to grow in unity and love with all your people everywhere.Amen.

Notes on use of this service, including dates, occasions and possible changes.

Making Miracles

Call

God, give the rulers of nations your justice and give righteousness to governments on earth, that they may rule your people rightly, and govern the poor with justice.

Prayer

Lord God, may your mercy be like rain that falls on the fields, like showers watering the thirsty soil. May justice come down like mighty waters, and may peace come like sunlight on the plains. Blessed be you, O Lord God of Israel. Blessed be your name, O ruler of the church and the world. May the whole earth be filled with your joy. Amen.

Scripture Reading

Amos 8:4-9   Luke 9:10-17

Suggested Hymns

156,   299

It is almost impossible for us to imagine the difference between our lives and those of most people in the Third World. Perhaps some in this group have experienced life in an underdeveloped nation. ((If so, you may wish to them share it with the group at this time)).

One person recently returned from a church-sponsored trip to Africa and told of visiting a small village just outside Lusaka in Zambia. The villagers lived under what to them were normal conditions, not in great need. An old woman invited the visitors to see her new cookhouse, attached to the straw home in which she lived. To the visitor

it looked like the kind of snowfort his children would throw together for a snowball battle. It was crudely fashioned of hand-made bricks in a rudimentary manner. Yet it was a source of pride for the whole village. The impression was not so much of poverty as of incredible simplicity. For them this simple structure represented progress and wealth.

Only for a very short time now will the people of that village regard such simple change as being notable. Only for a short time will they take for granted that the nations of the north are fated to have wealth while they are fated for poverty. Development is becoming an issue for us and for them.

A few years ago strong leaders like Lady Barbara Ward held out great dreams for the Decade of Development. She asked the developed nations to aim at giving at least 2% of the gross national product (GNP) for the development of the underdeveloped nations. The dreams died.

"Aid" is not enough. Only new froms of international trade agreements will allow necesssary growth in the underdeveloped areas. Yet every international meeting to effect such changes continues to be obstructed by wealthy nations, unwilling to accept less for themselves.

To some, these considerations may seem a long distance from faith in Christ. Not so. As one Christian thinker put it, "To be concerned about my own bread is materialist; to be concerned about my brother's bread is spiritual." In First John we read, "If a man has enough to live on, and yet when he sees his brother in need, shuts up his heart against him, how can it be said that love for God dwells in him?"

We talk about Christian love as "creative outgoing good will for other persons, but especially for those in need." Jesus told stories to illustrate such love. He told about a Samaritan (an outcast in Israel, almost like the untouchables of India). This man showed love by risking his life, by financial generosity, by giving valuable time, all for the sake of a man who despised the very word "Samaritan". Love means active caring. It means bread.

Archbishop William Temple pointed out that we all pray each Sunday, for our daily bread. The use of the plural commits us, each time we say the Lord's Prayer, to deep spiritual concern for the needy of the world.

Today serious committment means that we take some responsibility for the rules of the game in international trade. Most church members are not in a position to make such decisions, but they vote for those who do. We carry this responsibility into our offices and conferences, into management meetings, and riding meetings, into party conventions and church gatherings.

Archbishop Helder Camara of Brazil has written,
A poverty so degrading and a wealth so irresponsible are in blatant contrast to all the precepts of the scriptures. When shall we have the courage to outgrow the charity mentality and see that at the bottom of all
relations between rich and poor there is a problem of justice?

Only when we take such words seriously can we avoid discomfort each time we hear the Samaritan story.

Prayer
Bless the rich, O Lord, that they may be generous for others. Bless the poor, that they may be freed from poverty and stand with dignity in your presence and in the presence of your family. Bless the healthy, that their strength may benefit the community of humankind. Bless the weak that they may know the healing power of your love. We ask it in Jesus' name. Amen.

Notes on use of this service, including dates, occasions and possible changes.

Lydia

Call

One generation shall laud your works to another, O God, and shall declare your mighty acts. Our souls wait for you, O Lord, for you alone are our help and our shield.

Prayer

Your gentleness, O God, is like the sun, seeking to cheer and warm the hearts of humankind. Your goodness through all our days, is like bread and wine, increasing and renewing our strength within us. Your call is like the rain, refreshing us with new hope and truth. For all of these we give you thanks, in Jesus name. Amen.

Scripture Reading

Acts 16:9-19; 35-40.

Suggested Hymns

88 (Suggest changing v. 2, l. 3 - God who names us   295 (suggested alternate tune 344)

Who was Lydia? The first Christian convert in Europe, a woman!

Paul and his companions were carrying out an extensive mission to what we would now call Asia Minor. Paul became ill, probably from malaria. He was attended by a Greek doctor, Luke, who soon after became a Christian and was baptized. While they rested in Troy, Paul had a dream of a man from Macedonia calling to him, "Come over to us". Paul took his dream seriously. The man in the dream was likely his boyhood idol, Alexander the Great, whose home was Phillipi in Macedonia.

The friends crossed the Aegean and made their way to Phillipi. They found a group of women worshipping on the Sabbath by the river side. The worship was led by a woman named Lydia. Paul spoke to them and they, too, asked to be baptized as Christians. Later they met in the home of Lydia, their leader making it the first church in Europe.

This first European Christian was a fascinating woman. Her lifestyle was intriguing, for her day or ours. A successful businesswoman, she traded in dye and dyed goods. Purple was her "specialty", a colour of fabric that few could then afford. She probably had a love for texture and design in fabric.

One might question, "Why did the little group of women worship out of doors?" and "Why did they move into Lydia's home?" Women were not allowed into Jewish places of worship at the time. While these women may have been Gentile, it is clear that they had been influenced by Jewish neighbours and were observing the custom that forbade women in places of worship. Paul, with breadth of outlook, encouraged them to gather in a home.

Much of the credit must go to Lydia who obviously impressed Paul and his companions with her strong leadership. She was able to win the support of others and was willing to take risks for new ideas despite the fact that her commercial success might have been placed in jeopardy. She was a practical organizer and was generous and hospitable. She was plucky, brainy, risking, orginal and loving. An astonishing woman. Paul was pleased to validate her leaderhsip in Phillipi.

Lydia gets only brief notice in the book of Acts, yet she stands for a supremely important reality - the place granted strong and capable women in the church's earliest years.

If the scriptures give her a minimum of notice, the later histories of the early church give her and other strong women even less attention. Women seem almost invisible in the church's historical writings. Yet they were there from the start. Church history began when a small band of women set out to pay their last respects to a fallen friend. It began when, contrary to all reason, they publicly declared themselves followers of Jesus. His male friends, meanwhile, were in hiding. It was to women that the risen Christ was first revealed and they searched out the hidden men to bring them the good news.

Church history, ever since, has largely ignored its women. Most people who attend church today were introduced to faith by their mothers, yet many will blithely, and with straight faces, stand and sing, "Faith of our Fathers living still."

Lydia stands as a symbol of those women who want their faith first hand, not second hand through their "men-folk."

With women like Lydia and men like Paul we can say "yes" to the New Woman, and at the same time to the importance of the home; yes to the divinely intriguing difference between men and women and at the same time to laws which provide equal pay for equal work; yes to enduring marriages, grounded in a thought-out committment to one another, and at the same time to collegial family life where father may at times be the homemaking parent and mother the breadwinner or public figure.

We could wish for every descendant of Lydia her femininity but also her tough determination to lead. We could wish,too, that those qualities might receive recognition in the church without all the pain and ambiguity, resentment and lonliness that many daughters of Lydia have suffered along the way.

Prayer
O God of mercy and tenderness, but God also of strength and vision, we ask your presence with all who seek to understand the changes and newness that surrounds our lives. We are grateful for those who have been sensitive enough to your leading to risk disfavour while they followed the comnviction they believed were your gifts to them. Keep us open to new ways of dealing with life that more of your people may know the joy of accomplishment and fulfillment, through Christ we pray. Amen.

Notes on use of this service, including dates, occasions and possible changes.

Love God

Call

Praise the Lord all nations! Extol him all peoples! For great is his steadfast love toward us; and the faithfulness of the Lord endures forever.

Prayer

Lord Most High, we hold you in awe, for you are King over all the earth and Lord of our lives. We confess before you that we have ignored your Lordship, and followed other Gods. We have folowed the desires of our own hearts, instead of seeking the desire of yours. Forgive, cleanse, renew and redirect our lives, we pray. Amen.

Scripture Reading

Exodus 20:1-11   Luke 10:25-27

Suggested Hymns

30,   27

The first and greatest commandment is to love God. The first thing to recognize is that to love God is more than to believe in God, which in its turn is more than "believing that there is a God".

Clergypersons are often assailed by people who claim that they believe in God as if it were a virtue. The New Testament asnwer is "so does the devil"! The mental gymnastics for such bald belief are similar to those involved in believing in The Loch Ness monster, the Abominable Snowman or Ogopogo.

Loving God is something else. Jesus is not talking about a mental state; he is talking about a relationship. But how does one love God. Loving another human being who can be heard, seen and touched, presents difficulties enough. How does one love the unseen and unheard?

How does one love any other? By revelling in the company of the other, by being sensitive to the desires of the other, by responding with appreciation to the other.

We revel in the presence of God knowing that countless truly satisfying and fulfilling experiences are momentary encounters with God. "A haze on the far horizon, the touch of the goldenrod. Some of us call it autumn; others call it 'God'." Those who have learned to call it God find God's presence in every touch of beauty. Marjory Holmes prays, "Oh God, my God, when the winds cry I hear you, when the birds call I hear you, when the sea rushes in, it is like the rushing of my being towards yours."

At other times the touch of God's presence comes as a comforting word in a season of sadness, in the thrill of mastering a difficult step in Scottish dancing or a hot dog maneuvre on skis. It comes in the persistent demands for a change of heart that surge from deep within. It comes with the confidence of a presence as we walk through the valley of the shadow. It comes with the respite of peace after almost unendurable effort.

For a moment the glory flashes and is gone, but in that moment the plains of the commonplace have been lit with the glory of a presence that leaves a residue of awe and wonder for ever after. "Surely the Lord was in this place and I knew it not."

We show our love to God by appreciating and celebrating those moments. God touches our lives and we respond - sometimes with joy and gratitude, sometimes with confession and repentance, sometimes with a renewal of promises to ourselves and to God, sometimes with determination to act for others, sometimes with overflowing praise.

When those experiences have overtaken us, when we have known what it is to be found by God, then we see all of life through the eyes of love. We have no wish to subdue the glow of it, or put it off with some neat explanation in psychological jargon. We. treasure it, knowing that the reality of God's presence is life's finest gift, sweeter than wine and brighter than the sun.

Dag Hammerskold, one of the greatest diplomats and peacemakers of our century, kept his life with God hidden, until after his tragic death it was revealed in his journal. He writes,

God does not die on the day we cease to believe in a personal deity, but we die ... when our lives cease to be illumined by the steady radiance, renewed daily, of a wonder, the source of which is beyond all reason.

To love God is to revel in his presence and show our appreciation for it. John Donne expressed his love in powerful poetry:
Batter my heart, three-personed God, for you
As yet but knock, breathe, shine, and

seek to mend.
That I may rise and stand, overthrow me, and bend
Your force to break, blow, burn and make me new.

Prayer

O God, we celebrate your gift of love. We thank you that you have written into our deepest being chords that respond to your love and to the love of others. We thank you for common causes, shared appreciation, mutual responsibilities, for all that builds bonds of affection. In our rejoicing we pray for all who are unaware of your loving care, for all who feel deprived of affection, for all who have known the warmth of shared love but now must live alone, those who have felt love curdle and sour, those who feel solitary in their last years. Bless them all. Amen.

Notes on use of this service, including dates, occasions and possible changes.

Love Neighbour

Call
Behold how good and pleasant it is when brothers and sisters dwell in unity.

Prayer
Eternal God, our Judge and our Redeemer, we have not always dwelt in unity with our brothers and sisters. We have lived too much to ourselves, and too little for others. We have refused to shoulder the troubles of our friends and have turned our backs on our neighbour's needs. We have ignored the pain of the world and have passed by the hungry, the oppressed and the poor, without compassion or imagination. Forgive us, we pray. Release us from bondage to our own selfish interests and help us to follow Him who taught us to love our neighbours. In his name we ask it. Amen.

Scripture Reading
Luke 10:25-37

Suggested Hymns
213 (suggested tune 332)   216

Can we summarize the Christian life in a few words? Sure!! Jesus did it for us. Love God. Love your neighbour. Love yourself. We would add, from the perspective of the years since then, love Jesus.

But who is my neighbour? That question has a familiar ring. Jesus answered it in the passage that we read today, the story of the Good Samaritan. Jesus has a good deal to tell us in this one simple story but one central truth rings through it all. The neighbour we are to love is anyone who has needs that we can meet. It is that simple. Yet there is more complexity to that cornerstone statement than one might imagine.

At the level of meeting one-to-one need, most of us do not do badly. It is in our blood to be helpful, kind, merciful, to people whose need is obvious. Though we hear stories of traffic victims or others ignored by the crowd we still are shocked when we hear them. It is not what we expect of others or ourselves. There is no substitute for this immediate and direct care for those in need.

If Jesus were telling the story today, however, he might make some modifications. The Good Samaritan might raise some embarassing questions about the policing along the Jericho Road. (Could it be that the local highway patrol is getting some large donations to the Police Benefit Fund from the local bandits?). The Samaritan might well find his way onto the Mayor's Committee on Crime. He might be asking about the kind of ambulance service available to that part of the road compared with that given closer to the city. He might start a campaign to arouse public awareness of the need to report similar incidents by CB radio. He might also drop a note to the local bishop noting the failure of two professional ministers to offer care.

Jesus, in our situation, would probably talk about the fabric of society - our need to take seriously our social responsibilities.

This broad view was not a possibility in his day.

A cheap stereo receiver provides signals only from nearbytransmitters. A good set picks out of the ether signals from farther away. The contemporary Christian is one who picks up signals of need from a long way off. They may be thin and crackly but the Christian is tuned to them. The love of neighbour is as intimate as the care given by the Samartian. It is also, in our day, a love that stretches out across oceans and deserts and deep green forests into the hearts and lives of needy men, women and children around the world.

Arthur Stringer, a Canadian novelist whose work in prose gained him little fame, left a scrap of poetry that has immortalized him.

I have sought beauty through the dust of strife,
And sought meaning for the ancient ache,
And music in the grinding wheels of life;
Long have I sought and little found as yet
Beyond this truth: that love alone can make
Earth beautiful, and life without regret.

The Christian love of neighbour teaches us that every least person is a son or daughter of God,deserving dignity and opportunity and that all that destroys dignity and denies opportunity must be opposed by the disciples of Jesus.

Christian love teaches that God takes the talent and character, the drive and ability, of the strong and uses them to care for the weak.

Christian love sees how easily the love of neighbour is sacrificed to greed, how easily our best intentions are subdued by lust for power, glory and possession

The love of neighbour is to know all this and, inspired by this insight, to let the love of God work in us and through us.

Prayer
We bring to you, O God, the troubles and perils of peoples and nations. We recall the suffering of prisoners and captives, many whose fate is not of their own making. We think of the sorrow of the bereaved, the loneliness of strangers, the despair of those enslaved by habit, the helplessness of the oppressed, the weariness of those who work too hard and too long for too little, the anxiety of parents who must watch young people make their own mistakes, the bewilderment of young people watching the mistakes of their parents. For all of these we pray, O God. Amen.

Notes on use of this service, including dates, occasions and possible changes.

Love Yourself

This is the day that the Lord has made. Let us rejoice and be glad in it.

Prayer
We give you thanks, O god, that as we gather we know ourselves to be among friends. We thank you for the encouragement and understanding that they bring to our lives. We thank you above all, though, for the presence of Jesus, in whom is fullness of understanding and the richest of encouragement. In his name, we pray. Amen.

Scripture Reading
Ephesians 4:11-16

Suggested Hymns
319, 293

How often have we heard the Christian life summed up in what has been called "Jesus' Two-fold Commandment" - love God, love your neighbour. Such a summary ignores the fact that there was a third party in Jesus' words. "Love your neighbour as yourself" Love your neighbour as you have already learned to love yourself. He seems to imply that self love is already present as a model for love of the neighbour.

Many still have trouble with the notion of loving themselves. A couple of curious facts may help. We feel that loving oneself is somehow wrong, yet we feel distressed, hurt and even angry, when others don't love us. Are they not simply confirming our own judgement? Should we not applaud their wisdom?

We feel, as well, that we should love God and be grateful to him. We are impressed with his handiwork - all but the work done on us. We seem to say, You've done a great job on all the rest of creation, God, but you sure "blew it" on this item!!

These seem silly and frivolous approaches, yet they point to something serious.

Our problem with loving ourselves comes when we confuse it with selfishness, self-centeredness or conceit. Actually, selfishness is to self-love what infatuation is to true love - a distortion. If egotistical people truly loved themselves would they have to spend so much time convincing us of their worth? Bragging is a sure sign of insecurity not of healthy self respect.

On the other hand the classic "selfless" person has some problems. She often hides her lack of self esteem by giving herself completely to others. C.S. Lewis comments, "You can tell 'the others' by the hunted look.!"

In fact it is impossible to truly love another until we love ourselves. Without a proper love of self we lack the confidence to reach out to others.

Jesus advises us to be humble. But to be humble is not to think little of oneself. It is to see oneself with clear eyes, to see all one's strengths and talents, and to enjoy them, but as well we see how far we have yet to grow before we reach the stature of the fullness of Christ. To be humble is to stand tip-toe at full strength, exultant in all our powers, yet seeing the example of Christ still towering above us.

Carl Rogers, looking back over a lifetime as a world-class therapist could write, "Self love is not found in boasting or self-assertion, but rather in a quiet pleasure in being one's own self."
e.e. cummings has a delightful poem that is a hymn to individuality. It is called *Personality. Musings of a Police Reporter in the Identification Bureau*

You have loved forty women, but you have only one thumb.
You have a hundred secret lives but you mark only one thumb.
You go round the world and fight in a thousand wars
and win all the world's honours,
but when you come back home, the print of the one thumb your mother gave you is the same print of thumb you had in the old house where your mother
kissed you and said goodbye.
Out of the whirling womb of time come millions of men
and their feet crowd the earth and they cut one another's throats for room to stand
and among them there are not two thumbs alike.

Somewhere is a Great God of Thumbs who can tell the inside story on this.
Self-love, then, is simply the God-given enjoyment of one's God-given uniqueness and integrity.

Prayer
God, you are giver of all gifts. Today we would thank you for ourselves; for the bodies we enjoy; for legs that can walk, run,kneel and jump; for arms that can throw and hug, and reach out and touch; for eyes to see the first touches of green on spring trees; for ears to hear the high honking of returning geese; for taste to enjoy maple syrup or spumoni ice cream; for minds that can wrestle with new ideas; but above all for feelings, the source of warmth and assurance for all of life. We are grateful,O God. Amen.

Notes on use of this service, including dates, occasions and possible changes.

Love Jesus

Call
Grace and peace be to you from God, the Creator and from our Lord, Jesus Christ.

Prayer
Lord Jesus, you have called us to follow but we have hung back, full of excuses, and fearful to take the step away from so much we enjoy. We are caught up in familar habits, jobs we can perform with confidence, friendships that no longer take an effort. To follow you is to venture into the new and unknown, and we value our comfort and security. You must understand. It has always been this way. Yet we sense the tug of adventure also, and we feel the warmth of your love, and we would follow. Draw us to you we pray, for our sakes and for your own. Amen.

Scripture Reading
Ephesians 6:10-24

Suggested Hymns
107, 109

Many church members have spent time at camp when young. There are camp songs that still stir memories when old campers gather. Few have as much impact as "We are Climbing Jacob's Ladder." In one version the verse occurs. "Sinner, do you love my Jesus?"

One wonders how many campers asked themselves what it means to "love Jesus".

Jesus asked his followers to love God, to love their neighbour, and to love themselves. Those three loves every Christian shares with Jesus. They were the bedrock of his own life of faith. Christians share them also with people of conviction in any religious faith. Love of neighbour is shared with all humane people the world over.

But with this fourth love the Christian steps out of line and becomes unique. "Christian, do you love my Jesus?"

Here is the distinctive Christian note. In this person - a small town Jewish carpenter turned wandering preacher, who lived 2,000 years ago in what is now Israel, and who was executed as a criminal under Roman jurisdiction, - in this person was all of God that can be contained within the limitations of a human personality.

For the Christian to love God is to love God as seen in Jesus. To love the neighbour is to love the one whom Jesus made clear to be our neighbour. To love oneself is to love the one whom Jesus so loved that he would go to his death for that person.

The Christian life does not flow out of the imposition on life of a set of rules, nor even a set of beliefs about God, but flows from a personal love and loyalty for Jesus of Nazareth.

To love Jesus is to take up our cross and follow. The cross is not a tragedy laid on us by life without our permission, as common speech would have it. Our cross is our share of "the burden of the world's divine regret" which we voluntarily accept in order to take up some of Christ's load. That camp song goes on, "If you love him why not serve him?". We serve him by joining him as he serves the world.

Ralph Sockman once observed, "The richest spirits I know are those whose lives have experienced difficult times, while the sourest critics of my acquaintance have, on the surface of things, seemed to have had what seemed a sweet time of it. It is a fact of history that the literature of hope has come out of an environment of burdens and crosses, and the literature of pessimism has been written in circles of comfort and prosperity."

Blessed are the sorrow bearers, the burden bearers, for they shall be comforted. Percy Hayward, a YMCA worker, wrote a set of prayers for young people that included one to go with these thoughts. "Lord, push me out deep; I can't swim till I'm in deep water: give me a load to lift; I can't build muscles lifting feathers."

The strange paradox to which the love of Jesus leads us is that in carrying the cross we find joy. Dr. William Osler, world reknowned in his own time, had one patient he visited often. Her name was Jane, she was a little girl, and she was dying. The great man would come into her room in a crouching position, imitating a gnome, and in a squeaky voice would ask her, his fairy godmother, to give him some tea. He always said "It is my joy to come."

The joy, for the Christian, is in the sure knowledge that we never walk alone. "Lo, I am with you always." Christ does not remove burdens. He shares them. In sharing his is our love.

Prayer

Great God, though we pray for your coming, we know also that you have come. All human history is the story of your coming, and you are with us now. From the hour when your spirit stirred the dark deeps and called forth light, till your firstborn, clothed in light, called all humankind to follow, you have been touching and turning your world. And yet we wait. Strange hopes stir in our hearts. Can there be another birth? Another rising? Come like Easter morning again, O god, scattering darkness and doubt, lifting up hopes and happiness, till we rise, and shine and give you glory, now and forever. Amen.

Notes on use of this service, including dates, occasions and possible changes.

Love Your Enemies

Call

Be strong and of good courage; do not fear or be in dread, for it is the Lord your God who goes with you, and will not fail you or forsake you.

Prayer

Eternal God, in whose sight a thousand years are as an evening past, you number all generations, peoples and races among your family. As you have led our forebearers through the centuries, and as you have led us through the years, so guide us now that our hearts may seek your will and our resolves be strengthened by your love. Then may our loves be made broad and firm through Christ, Amen.

Scripture Reading

Genesis 37:1-11   Matthew 5:43-48

Suggested Hymns

27, 278

"You have heard it said that you shall love your neighbour and hate your enemy, but I say to love your enemies and pray for those who persecute you."

These are tough words for a tough thought.

Ours is a good time to hear them again. We lived in a time of increasing emnity. The lines are being sharply drawn and "polarity" is one of the watchwords of our day. Movements that once provided hope of unity are no longer in fashion - the U.N.. the ecumenical movement. Our national leaders favouor the rheto-

ric of separation. We all seem to lack a capacity for self-criticism yet over-react to criticism from others.

It is a far cry from Jesus' words about loving our enemies. It is interesting that Jesus says little else about enemies. The idea seems not to occupy him. The gospels record Jesus using the word only five other times,twice in the parables, once in quoting the Hebrew scriptures and twice in speaking of the forces of evil.

This one use of the word, though, is at the very heart of his teaching. "Love your enemies". What kind of counsel is this? Many would regard it as subversive if taken seriously. Would it not undermine the legal system and subvert the defense department? Even on a more personal level, are we to become doormats to every bully we meet?

An illustration at a personal level may help. You live with a room-mate. Some regulation is essential. But your roommate is a "messer". You become irritated, then angry, even mean.

You may be helped by looking at the room-mate from another angle. Perhaps, though a slob, she is a good-natured companion, can repair things, makes a great fettucini alfredo. Suppose, however, you discover nothing likeable about her. She has no redeeming social value!

There is one perspective left. Here is a child of God,loved by God. Difficult as this person is, annoying and provoking, she is still one for whom Christ died.

You see what has happened with this very significant shift. The room-mate is no longer the central figure in your thinking - God is. God is the pivot-point of life for each of you. You and this disturbing person beoth revolve around God. When that comes home to our hearts, quietly, mysteriously, everything shifts. What can I do to see that God does not love this person in vain? I do not have to submit to her mess. My own standards are unaltered. What is changed is the way I see, and therefore deal with, the other. To go well beyond the illustration, the love of God, who loves us, helps us to love the neighbour, who may even be the enemy. This runs much deeper than the familiar line about hating the sin but loving the sinner. The love of the enemy is present in the Old Testament figure of Joseph. The story-tellers painted an unpleasant picture both of Joseph and of his brothers. He was a vain brat;they were brutal schemers. But when the moment of truth arrived, what might have been Joseph's day of revenge became, instead, a day of joyous reunion. "Fear not", says Joseph. Am I in the place of God?" He does not judge, he does not hate. He creatively loves his enemies. It is risky. They could have done him in again. He was prepared to risk.

Outlandish as it sounds, it may be that the same attitude is our best hope in international affairs. When the space race was heating up the emnity between the Soviets and the West Hugh McLennan wrote a telling essay in a national magazine.
"I believe it is essential not to be so afraid of death as we are now, not to be so aggressive as we are now, not to be so full of hate and fear as we are now.... I think we should stop hating the Russians in our propaganda, that we should stop hating the Russians altogether. If the worst comes to the worst we should ask ourselves the question, 'Do we prefer to die like Christians or like terrified hysterics?' And I believe that if we answer that question properly wisdom will come, and after wisdom that mysterious defender of our ancestors, the Grace of God."

Prayer

O Lord, you have given us a hard commandment, to love our enemies. We trust that you do not ask that which is beyond our capacity. So we ask that the love which flows from you, may so fill us and direct us, that those whom we meet may feel its warmth and turn to you for the peace and harmony that only you can give. We ask it in Jesus' Name. Amen.

Notes on use of this service, including dates, occasions and possible changes.

61

Butterflies Are Free

Call

Christ our Passover is sacrificed for us: therefore let us keep the feast. Christ is risen from the dead, and become the first fruits of them that slept.

Prayer

This week, O God, we celebrate the joy of Easter. In the rising of your son we find new hope and purpose for all that we do and are. The dark hours of Good Friday are behind us, the road opens into sunlight ahead, and we walk with confidence that our hopes are not in vain. Walk with us, then, O God, as Jesus walked with his friends along the roads of Galilee. Teach us your way. Heal our weak wills. Share with us your own dream for your world, that we may enter into it with fresh hope and joy in this season of new beginnings. Amen.

Scripture Reading

John 19:38-42   20:1-18

Suggested Hymns

465,   468

The Monarch butterfly is a summer favorite, with its brown and orange colouring and intricate designs. It is hard to imagine that this frail creature battles buffeting winds and storms to migrate, like the birds, in the autumn. Its wings beat so slowly and lightly it seems impossible that it can cover the thousands of miles to its winter grounds. Yet for years tourists have visited Pacific Grove, near Monterey, Califonia to see the monarch butterflys clustering on the branches of an avenue of "butterfly trees" creating their own golden foliage.

Recently Toronto naturalist, Fred Urquart, discovered the winter home of the eastern Monarch butterflies, in the Sierra Madre mountain range, 150 miles from Mexico City. On his first view one fell at his feet from a branch, and on its wing was a tiny label, "Send to Zoology, U of T." He had placed the tag himself!! What an incredible thrill of discovery. All had fallen into place, including his own name.

It is the same sort of thrill one experiences in discovering the perfect symbol, - like the butterfly for Easter - the "perfect fit".

In one church, at Easter a banner showed a caterpillar looking over his shoulder with a quizzical air, and the caption read "Change! Who me!!" Similarly, a cartoon pictures two caterpillars walking together with a butterfly hovering overhead. One caterpillar turns to the other and says, "Boy, you'll never catch me up in one of those things.!" For Easter the significant realization is that there is nothing wrong with being a caterpillar except .... except that the caterpillar could have become a butterfly!!

The butterfly speaks of Easter and of life. God has written into our lives stages in growth just as he has into the caterpillar that evolves into the butterfly. There is in all living nature a propulsion to grow. The butterfly's stages of growth may be more dramatic than ours, yet we do change with the years. Our bodies grow and change, of course, but our souls likewise develop. There is, however, a perculiarly human capacity to resist that growth of spirit, to shrink back, to want it to be too easy.

In Charles Dicken's novel, *Bleak House* one character says, "I only ask to be free. The butterflies are free. Mankind will surely not deny to Harold Skimpole what it concedes to the butterflies." Skimpole is impatient. It takes time to go through each stage, and the going is never free. It is costly in wear and tear on the psyche. Yet the meaning of life is that we do move through those stages, growing as we go.

A play and movie borrow Dicken's line, *Butterflies Are Free*. The story is about a young blind man, Don, who falls in love with a sighted girl in the next appartment, Jill. She loves him but is fearful of a lasting relationship. He handles his disability well but knows that his freedom would expand in a loving relationship. The rest of the play is Don's struggle to find more freedom, discovering along the way that in many ways he is more free than Jill, his friend. It is a delightful story yet there is a sadness about it because the human dimension is the only one in which the two young people work. They miss the real message of the butterfly which is that God gives us another whole dimension of life if we will yeild ourselves to his process. The butterfly has no choice. We have.

We can choose to let the spirit of God grant us rebirth. The energy crisis is not just a national problem, but a personal one. God gives to those who ask and are open power to become new creatures.

The same message of growth and change that holds for life holds, also, for death. The butterfly's chrysalis is a kind of death. Yet new life springs from the old, new powers allow the new creation to shed the old body and emerge in new beauty.

What a perfect Easter symbol the butterfly is! New life for old. In his new life Jesus said, "I go to prepare a place for you... and you ... and you.

Prayer

Thanks be to you, O God, for victory, through our Lord Jesus Christ whom you raised for us all. Raise us, too, to newness of life. Help us to shed the dry binding of selfishness or abuse, of lonliness or weariness. May we rise to a life of freedom, of giving, of caring. Then, in your good time, may we know the total freedom of life with you, life without the restraints of time and place, all in the glory of your presence. These are the hopes we bring in the spirit of Easter. Amen.

Notes on use of this service, including dates, occasions and possible changes.

The Morning After

Call

The scriptures tell us, Work out your salvation with fear and trembling,for it is the Spirit of the Lord that works in you.

Prayer

Almighty God unto whom all hearts are open and from whom no secrets are hid, cleanse the thoughts of our hearts by the inspiration of your Holy Spirit, that we may worthily praise you and serve you through Christ our Lord. Amen.

Scripture Reading

Phillipians 2:1-7; 12-18

Suggested Hymns

253, 262 (to the same tune as 253 - a little tricky but worth the effort of putting the words to the music)

In the gospel according to Saint John there is a fascinating after-Easter story. Peter, Thomas, Nathanel and the brothers James and John are back home in Galilee. Jesus has risen. They have seen him. Now what are they to do? What does one do post-resurrection?!

When in doubt, try the familiar. They go fishing. They fish all night and as they pull for shore they see Jesus at the lakeside, making breakfast. What does one do after a resurrection? What does one do for an encore? One fries fish for hungry fishermen! That is, one goes back to the old familar routine. Has nothing changed, then? Not likely!! Yet, what is different?   Same lake, same beach, same fish, same fishermen.

But now it is all seen through Easter eyes. These people would never look at life the same way again. Graduation from resurrection does not mean entry into some new world, some new form of existence. It means life will look familar but will feel quite different.

The misty lake, with the green hills that roll back from the shore, and rich blue sky above, are all familiar. The smell of the boney little fish frying. All this they had known all their lives. Now, it is all different because the tall, bronzed young man who bends across the fire, has made everything different. He has given them, eyes to see and ears to hear, as he said he would. All must be used in the real world they have known since birth.

Too often people try to appeal for religious faith by looking to the unnatural. They appeal to miracle, to other-worldly experiences. God, the Great Coincidence, is effectively pushed out of daily living although he planted himself firmly there in the Incarnation.The smell of fresh frying fish for breakfast gives the messsage that God is to be discovered in the commonplace.

After breakfast, Jesus took Peter aside for one of the most moving conversations in the gospels. One must know that there are a number of Greek words for our English word love. A deep and intimate friendship is philia. But the word that the New Testament uses for the distinct self-giving, outgoing, good will we are asked to offer to our neighbour is agape. Some feel that only God is capable of agape-love.

These distinctions must be appreciated to feel the subtle nuances of this conversation which, in English, often seems a strange repetitive kind of dialogue. Jesus says to Peter. "Peter, do you love (agape) me?" Peter, remembering his brash promises of love, and remembering the cock-crow that marked his denial of those promises, can reply only, "Lord, you know I philia you." "Feed my sheep", says Jesus, but then he returns to his question, "Peter, do you agape me?" Peter is clearly perturbed, but probably not by Jesus' questions so much as by his own inability to answer as he knows Jesus would wish. He will not promise more than he can deliver. Wretched because he can say no more, he will only reply, "Lord, I philia you". "Feed my lambs", says Jesus. But he is not done. Peter must have caught his breathe in near despair as Jesus framed the question a third time. "Peter, do you philia me?" With what must have been a shout of joy, Peter could respond, Lord you know I philia you!!"

Jesus might have wished for more. Yet, he would take Peter where he was, demanding no more, but taking him on his own terms. "Feed my sheep" he said once more, with the firmness in his voice that must have recaptured some of the wonder of the day when he had told Peter, "You are a rock, and I can build a church on such a rock."

Though he had failed Jesus, Jesus did not fail him. He took a mortal man in a material setting - a person like us in a world like ours. That is the wonder of the incarnation. After the once- in-all-history event of Easter, God returned to ordinary people in ordinary settings to work his will.

Prayer

You are the maker of covenants, O Lord. You have been with us through the ages. You walked with us when we wandered as strangers in the world. You liberated us when captive. You lead us out of bondage. You sent us Jesus, our Master and Lord, that we might follow in his way and find abundant life. You have nourished us with your gifts of bread and wine. You have trusted us with his ministry in the world. In all these ways you have covenanted with your people to be our God if we will but be your people. Even when we have shunned, forgotten or ignored you, you have continued your love. Forgive us our failure, we pray, and renew your trust, that we may be the peole you had hoped would be, loyal disciples of Jesus, worthy children of the Most High. Amen.

Notes on use of this service, including dates, occasions and possible changes.

Ruth

Call

Wait for the Lord. Be strong, and let your heart take courage; Yea, wait for the Lord.

Prayer

O God, ever blessed, you have given us the night for rest and the day for service. Grant that the refreshment of the night may renew us in our search for your glory in the day. By your spirit, help us to turn disappointment into patience, success into gratitude, failure into learning, pleasure into praise, and criticism into growth, through Christ our Lord who has given us an example of just such a life. Amen.

Scripture Reading

Ruth 1:15-22   Matthew 1:1-5;17

Suggested Hymns

277 (suggested alternate tune 161)   274 If possible find a soloist who can sing Gounod's arrangement of the words from Ruth - "Entreat me not to leave Thee".

The Book of Ruth is an exquisite cameo of narrative storytelling. It is one of the great romances of world literature, but those who decided on the contents of the Bible must have seen more in it than literary merit alone. In this story of a gentle loving woman and wife, is a message for its own day and ours.

The three main characters in the story represent three attitudes to the "outsider". At the time of its writing an attitude of racial superiority had been adopted by some Jews especially in relation to immigrants in the land of Israel. Today much the same situation exists here as native Canadians resolve their feelings about newcomers to our land.

Naomi represents the best of those who stood for racial purity and for the exclusion of those of other races. She is a courageous, resourceful woman, but she lines up with those who want to keep Israel for the Israelites. Her sons have married women of other races and while she is disappointed she remains a gracious person.

Boaz, the Israelite farmer whom Ruth eventually meets and marries when her husband, Naomi's son, dies, is a dignified, strong, tolerant man of the soil. There is an air of confidence and grace about him that is most attractive.

Ruth is the completely good and admirable "foreigner". She is nice, in the nicest way, not "soppy" but genuinely, down to earth, caring about other people.

It is a story of a rare depth of friendship between mother-in-law and daughter-in-law, despite all Naomi's religious convictions about the superiority of her race. It is a story of loyalty, trust and devotion, under very difficult circumstances. The narrative breaks into six clear acts, each one depicting the way in which the leading characters care for one another with tenderness and thoughtfulness yet without sugary sweetness. As such it provides a model for all family living.

Behind this personal level of the story is the social significance. The compassion for one another exhibited in one-to-one caring must be carried out beyond the circle of family and friends to the community, and to the nation - and ultimately to the world of nations.

Taken to its ultimate end, for the Christian there can be no "foreigners", only people in a foreign land. "He has made of one blood all the nations of the earth". Dr. Helen Caldicott, the Australian peace activist says, "What can we do? We can right here and now learn to live as a family with those who seem most difficult."

It would be easy to discount the message in Ruth. Surely there are few people in our land who adopt that kind of attitude. for Such optimism is belied by the disturbing experience of listening to some of the late night phone-in broadcasts on radio and hearing the bitter hatred expressed by many. In a recent such show on the date in January designated as Martin Luther King Day a caller said, "I'm celebrating today. I'm celebrating James Earl Ray day. Thank God for what he did for America." It is easy to dismiss such a call as the lunatic fringe of fanaticism until one takes seriously how often such sentiments are expressed.

Eddie Murphy the black comedian who goes from triumph to triumph as probably the most assured box-office success of the decade, tells it, "I walk down the street in any city in the U.S. and people know who I am, but I can't get a good seat in some New York restaurants".

On this side of the border Canadians should have little difficulty making the connection between Ruth's story and that of a Cree or Blackfoot woman, or of a woman from Pakistan.

Ruth and Boaz had a child. That child, in time, became the grandfather of David, the King, the most highly respected leader in all Israel's history. "And born to us, of David's line, in the city of Bethlehem, a child" - a child with Moabite blood in his veins from his distant ancestor, Ruth. He became Elder Brother to us all, black, white, brown, yellow or red.

Prayer

In the midst of all our joys, O God, we feel sorrow and stress, pain and fear around us. We pray for all who suffer oppression because of the colour of their skin, the language they speak, the clothes they wear, the God they worship. We pray for those who feel lost and lonely in a strange land and pray that you will write a welcome into our hearts for Christ's sake Amen.

Notes on use of this service, including dates, occasions and possible changes.

Blessed Trinity

"Grace be to you from God the Father and from our Lord Jesus Christ". Not a surprising greeting in church! Yet this truly is a strange formula we've been using today - Father, Son and Spirit, or any of the more current forms - Creator, Redeemer, Guide. We have heard it so often it raises no questions in our minds. The over-all term Holy Trinity raises even fewer questions. It may be the name of a church you've belonged to, or a College your daughter is attending.

Years of usage have implanted these words in our vocabulary. Glory be to God the Father, and to the Son and to the Holy Spirit, Amen.

Try to write a paragraph explaining the notion of the Holy Trinity. If you do some research for such a paragraph you will be surprised to discover that the term is not to be found anywhere in the Bible!

First used 300 years after the death of Jesus, it came into the Christian vocabulary after a lengthy and fiery debate on how to form-ulate, find form for, what Christians had experienced. It did not arise from an airy debate by professors of theology on fine points of theory. It was the result of everyday Christians reaching consensus on how to put into words what they had shared in daily living.

How have we encountered God? How do we find words for our encounter with the deity? What appears to be the nature of God?

As they discussed the ways God had chosen to reveal the divine presences they found their thought gathering around three distinct categories. There is surely but one God, yet we have found God acting in three ways - three ways at least! God in three persons, blessed Trinity.

As soon as we use the word "person" we are in trouble. For the early Christians used the word in a different manner than we do. In Greek drama the Personna was the mask used by an actor to represent feelings. Thus we have the happy face and sad face as the logo for theatre today. Then the term was transferred to the actual "role" played - thus we find old playbills that list the "dramatis personnae" - the roles of the drama.

Now we are closer to the meaning. One God, yet three roles. A human analogy may help. Each of us plays at least three roles at home. One may arrive home, see the children playing ball hockey in the driveway, give each a pat on the shoulder and say "How's it going?" - the paternal role. One walks into the house a nd greets one's spouse with a fairly passionate kiss - the spousal role. Same person - different style of action. Then a mother-in-law or father-in-law may be sitting in the living room. One gives a kiss, but a more chaste one this time, the filial role. We are percieved in three roles, yet remain one.

So Go is not a unit but a union, not a unity but a community. There is in God, as in each of us, something that resembles a "society". Neither we nor God are single beings, living and loving alone. God, like us, yet in a magnitude we cannot imagine, is personal and loving. In the beginning God - but if God is love, then —in the beginning relationship.

Leo Rosten tells of the old Jewish fellow knocked down while crossing the street in front of a Cathedral. A priest seeing the accident rushed to him and fearing he might die, asked him, "Do you believe in God the Father, Son and Holy Spirit?" The old fellow gasped, "Oy,

I'm dying and he's asking me riddles!!" We may feel as dismayed in having to deal with fine points of theology at a time when there are many questions that seem more pressing. Yet our own response to life is shaped by our convic-

tions. As one made in God's image I am expected, like God, to be"creative, in community, for the sake of others." Doctrine so practical engages us and directs us.

Prayer
O God of all life, you are present to us in the wonder of creation; in the quiet whisper of a spring breeze and in the thunderstorms that shake the earth. You are present also in the tall strong son of Galilee, whose earthly life provides a pattern, whose death provides release from old captivities, whose rising awakens a fresh new hope.We know your presence, too, in the still small voice within that warns us when we stray from your ways, and encourages us when we might stop along the way. We are grateful for your coming in these ways. Amen.

Notes on use of this service, including dates, occasions and possible changes.

Handicaps

Call

For God alone, our souls wait in silence; from him comes our salvation. He is our rock and salvation, our fortress. We shall not be shaken.

Prayer

Our God, we thank you for work to do and skill to do it, for friends who share in the day, for the support of families and communities. All these we bring with us as we enter your presence. Now add to these the wonder of your word, the guidance of your spririt, and the assurance of your love, and our lives shall be full and free. In Jesus name we pray. Amen.

Scripture Reading

Genesis 45:4-8   Acts 16:6-10
Luke 22:39-44

Suggested Hymns

131 , 139

In golf we are asked, "What's your handicap?" Some of us may, when asked the question, feel tempted to pour out some of the frustrations we feel about our limitations.

As creatures endowed with sense, intellect, and imagination, yet fated to live for a limited number of years, weighted down with vulnerable bodies and minds, and in the midst of people and things which offer resistance to our purposes - limitations are inevitable!!

Our highest aims and fondest hopes are thwarted by the fact that we are temporary, tentative, inadequate and impatient.Our knowledge is fractional, our victories conditional, and our happiness fragile. In short we are people not Gods.

But here is the important fact. *We are well-loved children of God.* And that is our consolation prize for never being total winners in life. We can never be total losers either.

We have our limitations, our handicaps, each of us. Some have more than others. Yet we are often too quick to judge who has the most.

A human relations trainer, Mike LiSanti, was visiting a large corporation where he was hoping to obtain a contract. He was greeted at the front desk by a most gracious receptionist who asked if he would like a cup of coffee while he waited for Mr. Brown, who was a little delayed. The trainer happily assented. When the receptionist reached down, grasped the top of two wheels and swung back from the desk, Lis Santi was surprized to see her wheelchair. She propelled herself down to the hall, to return in a few minutes with his cofee. Shortly afterwards she led him down the hall to Mr. Brown's office, and deftly backed her wheelchair to allow him to enter. As soon as she was gone and LiSanti had exchanged greetings with Mr. Brown whom he had not met before, he commented on the extraordinary success that the receptionist had in dealing with her handicap.

"So, you think she's handicapped?" said

Mr. Brown. "Why, yes!" said the trainer. "Well, Mr. LiSanti," said the executive, reaching down at his sides to propel himself away from, his desk in his wheelchair, "Come with me." With that, he wheeled over to the window. "Tell me, Mr LiSanti, if your watch were to stop could you fix it." "Not at all" the trainer replied. "That's interesting," said Mr. Brown, enjoying himself. He gestured out the window to a large industrial buidling. "There are 300 people in there who could fix your watch, Mr. LiSanti. Each is in a wheelchair. I would say you handle yourself very well - considering your handicap!" The trainer got the contract but also gained an insight.

Each of us must accept the limitations that belong to our particular lives. For each of us there is agony and ecstasy. The ecstasy of creation and the agony of not being able to create as we would wish. Each of us is trying to create, learning to create better, and never succeeding in creating as we hoped to do. Each of us must, as Howard Thurman put it, "sit down with our tragic fact, and make friends with it". The great appeal of *Amadeus* as stage play and film was that it somehow gave a benediction for mediocrity and each of us could breathe a sigh of relief.

The moment of facing a limitation may be the moment God has been waiting for to open another door. James Whistler, the great painter, said, looking back on his dismissal from West Point, after a failure in his chemistry exam, "If silicone had been a gas I might have been a Major-General by now."

Our own limitations should make us especially sensitive to those whose limi-

tations are most obvious. On every page of the gospels we note that sensitivity. Watch Jesus healing physical afflictions then turning his attention to the limitations of the group who gathered round - those who were too blind to see the need for compassion. He speaks of God's banquet laid for the beggars, the crippled, the lame and the blind. This is the God of the oppressed at work in his world.

Prayer

God of tenderness and compassion, we would learn from you awareness of the needs around us. Keep before us, we pray, the sight of Jesus touching to new life those who had been unable to keep pace with the rest of the world. Make us sensitive to the disabled, - those who might use us as their eyes, those who live with the silent disability of deafness, those whose legs and backs can no longer carry the body through the routine joys of movement. We pray for the sick, the confined, the fearful, the anxious. We know that all human life flourishes like a flower of the field and is gone yet your mercy is from everlasting to everlasting. May we feel that mercy surrounding and guiding us now. Amen.

Notes on use of this service, including dates, occasions and possible changes.

Balcony or Basement

Call

The mighty one, God the Lord, speaks, and summons the earth. From the rising of the sun to its setting , our God comes.

Prayer

Eternal God, we bear your name, your imprint, when we are called Christian. We pray that this time of worship will help us to grow up into him who has given us his name. May we mirror his love, reflect his grace, and bear his stamp on our lives, to your glory. Amen.

Scripture Reading

1 Peter 2:11-17; 4:7-11

Suggested Hymns

30, 237

Are you a balcony person or a basement person?

Joyce Landorf, in her book, *Balcony People*, distinguishes the two. Balcony people, she says, are those who affirm others, lift them. Basement people on the other hand, drag people down, belittle them. There are many ways of dividing the people in the world - good and bad, sheep and goats, givers and grabbers, haves and have-nots. Balcony people and basement people is a new designation, and a helpful one.

Balcony people are the ones who encourage us when we have a new idea or plan. They are the ones who shout "Yeah!", "Right on!" "You can do it!" "Go for it!" At the same time the basement people are shouting, "What a dumb idea!", "We've tried that before!" "Are you kidding!".

Writes Landorf,"*I am sure, if there were a way to view a movie and see instant replays of all the strategic change points in our lives, that we'd instantly spot the people who either broke our spirits by their critical judgemental evaluations, or who healed us by their loving, perceptive affirmations.*"

The two texts from Peter tell the tale. He describes how Christians are expected to act towards one another. "Above all hold unfailing your love for one another." We remember that to love, in this sense, is not neccessarily to "like" but to care for.

All know the feeling of being respected, and all know, likewise, the feeling of being put down. Some recall being ridiculed as children in front of family or friends; others recall, as a spouse, being put down at a dinner party; or some may think of the time when an employer administered a dressing down with peers present. The world is overloaded with rejection mechanisms that make us feel judged, found wanting and condemned.

We are not dealing in thin theology here. This is not just another "be nice to others" talk. We are dealing, rather, with the heart of the gospel. What Peter is saying is that the love of God long ago dealt with all our inadequecies and frailties and with the failings of our fellows too. God loves us and them despite the many reasons why such love is unthinkable. Who are we, then, to stand in judgement of another?

Peter gives some other helpful directions. "Live as servants of God." How do we do that? "Honour all persons, love the brotherhood, revere God, honour the emperor." Concentrate for a moment on those first directives.

To honour another is to make space for the differences between us. It is not necessarily to agree with the other, but to take the other seriously. Encouragement is a major ingredient of the style that Peter is advocating here. That means not doing for another but encouraging the other to do for himself, herself. At a recent "roast" for a popular minister guest after guest rose to taunt the "victim" about the way he got them to do jobs for him. They laughed about his subtle methods of talking them into accepting various tasks, yet each acknowledged, with affection, how his prompting had resulted in personal development and growth. Balcony people are those who "honour" others, who take others seriously.

The difference between "balcony" and "basement" is probably never as significant as it is in parenting.

Children's author Jean Little, of Toronto, describes balcony parents delightfully in her book, *Hey, World, Here I Am.*

> In my family, we don't talk much about loving.
> My mother never bakes us pies or knits us socks. More than once she's put cream in my father's coffee, although he takes it black. When she gets home from work she collapses with her feet up. I have to shake her awake when its time to eat.
> My father never sends her roses or Valentines. He just says to her,'April, listen to this, April...' while he reads her something by E.B. White or Tolstoy.
> I listen too. And they listen when I find something so perfect it must be shared. Nobody ever says, 'Not now, I'm busy'.
> .....Loving isn't as simple as I once thought. Talking about it isn't what matters most."

Balcony people honour and respect.

Prayer

Our God, we are dazzled by your love for us the unworthy. We are humbled by your care. Yet even with this assurance burning in our hearts we are capable of coldness of heart and meaness of spirit to those around us. Draw us near to you, that your unfailing love may enlarge our hearts and your amazing grace brighten our spirits, through Christ our Lord. Amen.

Notes on use of this service, including dates, occasions and possible changes.

Compassion Burnout

Call
Our souls wait for the Lord. He is our help and our shield. Yea, our hearts are glad in him, because we trust in his holy name.

Prayer
Here we are. Lord, of good intentions but of inadequate action; of high hopes but of low power. And you, O Lord, are the one before whom all created things are as dust and vapour. Yet we dare to lift our hearts as we lift our voices, talking to you as children to a loving parent, for in Jesus we have known you to be so, and we rejoice. The marvel of your world causes us to rejoice, the tragedy of your world causes us to look to you for strength. So dwell with us now, O Lord, that our rejoicing and our seeking may be rewarded by your presence, through Christ our Lord. Amen.

Scripture Lesson
Deuteronomy 10:12-15; 17-21.
Matthew 25:31-40

Suggested Hymns
73, 274.

That Last Judgement scene is "awesome".

Who can hear it without asking, "Have I been merciful?" "Have I been merciful enough?"

Another disturbing scene is the familar one on TV - sunken faces of African children, fly-blown and glazed with death. The two scenes come together in our minds as we ask ourselves, "Have I been merciful enough?"

Such experiences nibble away at the edges of our joy, leaving us uneasy and guilty. How lavish the simple gifts we have brought for our children's birthdays would be in the eyes of those mothers of India who watch their babies wilt! How do I balance Christian concern for others with carrying on a life that is normal in my context? While I do give time, material gifts, and, above all, emotional energy, to concerns like these, how do I prevent being burned out by the limitless demands of a hungry, hurting world?

In a church newsletter the minister wrote, "Perhaps it is May-itis, but I notice in myself and others a kind of bedraggledness that seems to say, 'I would like to be concerned about global atrocities and all, but I don't have the energy. Commitment is hard work'" He is right. Commitment is hard work, and the result of that kind of work can be burnout - compassion burnout.

Burnout is a technical term turned popular. Normal fatigue can be cured with rest since it is mainly a physical state. Burnout is more complex, not just stress in new dress, but a form of emotional exhaustion that includes disenchantment, disillusionment, and sometimes anger. It comes from wearing oneself out in excessive striving towards unrealistic goals.

Many are feeling it today in connection

with the scenes we have pictured. Hopes have failed and ideals have died. Yet we feel compelled to care. What can we do? We can do six things.

1) We can get some perspective on our self-importance. Each person is important in God's plan, but no one person is all-important. We are expected to give to God's causes the "stubborn ounces of our weight" but in so doing we are not to mistake ourselves for Messiahs. We must learn to laugh at our own self-importance without putting ourselves down.

2) We can get some perspective on our "cause". Burnout is often linked with disappointment, and disillusionment. In the movie *Big Chill* a young attorney who entered law "to fight for the rights of oppressed" finds that he is defending "people who are often rotten and guilty as blazes".
Every good action is open to abuse. Christians, who operate with a recognition of the presence of Original Sin are less likely to be alarmed by the fact that not everyone assisted is an admirable person.

3) We can test our own motives. Only when we act for others because we recognize them as children of God and recognize that we are called by God to act on their behalf, only then are we likely to perservere. Service is not an obligation for the Christian; it is a calling. Disillusionment comes when we expect gratitude. The Christian asks only the assurance that this is God's will.

4) We can nurture a vision of the Kingdom of God. Paul advised, "Keep the vision given to you on the mountain".

We saturate ourselves in Christ's own vision. It might seem that we are back at the place where we are promoting burnout by holding up too high an ideal, but note that this is not the the starting place.

5) We can choose specific limited areas in which to act. Christians will often want to give their time and effort to a cause that is lesser known rather than to the high profile programmes with strong public appeal.

6) Finally, we can "wait on the Lord". Have you ever noticed that the famous lines from Isaiah, "They that wait upon the Lord ..." seem to move backwards. The natural climax would move from walking to flying. Isaiah knew that real-life enthusiasm starts with flight and ends with weary walking, yet even the walker who waits on the Lord shall not faint.

Prayer
Lord God, there are many who find our customary prayers of thanksgiving difficult. Around the world are those who face the prospect of death daily, and worse yet, the possibility of the death of their children. Others live in daily fear of arbitrary violence. We lift our hearts with our voices asking your love and care for all these your children, and we pray that you will make us generous with our resources of goods and time and talent. Amen.

Notes on use of this service, including dates, occasions and possible changes.

Saints Preserve Us

Call

Preserve us, O God, for in you do we place our trust. We will say to the Lord, "You are our God. We have no good apart from you."

Prayer

Lord Jesus, your mark is upon us. Your words haunt us. Your example is always before us. Your expectations spur us on. Your promises lure us. We cannot escape you even if we would. We place ourselves in your presence now to be grasped by your spirit and to be counted among your followers in all the world and in all time. Amen.

Scripture Reading

Luke 6:27-36

Suggested Hymns

148, 273

In the book of Genesis is a fascinating story of Abraham bargaining with God. The stakes are high!! He is bargaining for the preservation of a whole city.

God had become angry with the licentious behaviour in Sodom and had decided to destroy the city entirely. Abraham, with his usual compassion, had pity on the people. He entered into a lengthy session of haggling with God. What an astonishing picture this presents! Yet it is a procedure familiar to those who have visited the near east. It seems that all of life there is a process of negotiation.

Abraham asked, "How many good men

would it take (notice, it is always *men* at this stage in human history) for you to spare the city? How about fifty?!" God settled for fifty. But Abraham then began to work him down. "How about forty? Would you take thirty? Lets say twenty *really good* men!" Then the last word. "Oh, let the Lord be not angry and I will speak to yet this once more. Peradventure ten should be found there. Will you spare the city for ten?" One assumes a long dramatic pause, then God's words, uttered with a deep sigh. "I will not destroy it for the sake of ten."

As with most amusing, puzzling, colourful, Old Testament stories a life-truth lies hidden in the strange tale. The truly good may be few but they are a saving force.

The same truth is found in Jesus' familiar words. "You are the salt of the earth." His phrase has become part of our common language. One hardly thinks anything of it in saying that a friend or neighbour is "the salt of the earth". What does that mean?

What does salt do? A number of things, really. That is why it has been a highly prized commodity throughout history. For one thing, it adds flavour. Most soups, for example, would be dull without it. Jesus' followers add zest to the community.

It also prevents infection, keeps produce from rotting. It preserves goodness. Jesus is saying something about the way his followers purify and preserve the community. In this he is echoing the story of Abraham's ten men who preserved the city from destruction.

There are traces of Abraham's story in Jewish life still. The Jewish community reveres the "zaddick" - the righteous person, the one who graciously does good for others, and who loves God with a winsome spirit. They also tell of the "lemedh vovnik" - the hidden zaddickim. The people who do good so quietly that the community is not aware of their goodness. Legend says, it is the presence of these that keeps God's hand from destruction. As long as there are at least thrity-six such persons God will preserve his people. They are small in number but they preserve the community.

We would call them saints. And it is a solidly founded expression when we say, "Saints preserve us!" They do!
What is a saint, then - the one who is the salt of the earth - the hidden zaddickim

Most of the crowd who heard Jesus on the hill that day would never be known to more than a few people yet the master named them the salt of the earth.

The ten citizens of Sodom had names known only to their neighbours. The sainthood that preserves the community has little to do with fame. Peter Marshall the great American preacher of a generation ago spoke once about "The saints of the rank and file". If the saints can preserve us it will be just such saints as these.
There is a third significance to salt. It is essential; in preserving a balance of body chemicals. In this sense it preserves health. It is a fascinating fact that a number of very important English words, which may at first seem unrelated, spring from the same root in an earlier language - they are whole, healthy, hale and holy. The holy person is the healthy person, and true wholeness requires both health and holiness.

The saints are those who will keep the world whole, healthy and holy - in short, those who will preserve the world.

Prayer

Lord God of our Fathers and our Mothers, we come to you now as your followers have come to you through all time to praise, to wonder, to learn. We have walked through familiar streets, enjoying the gardens and the buildings along the way. It all seems so far removed from the Galilean hills, and the teeming market places of Jerusalem where our minds have been journeying. Yet, we feel one with those who heard the words of the Master for we share the same need for forgiveness and cleansing, for renewal and redirection, for gratitude and growth. In the stillness of worship we feel the centuries roll back and we know ourselves to be in the presence of the Maker and Shaper of the ends of the earth. So we would bring our thanks, and our prayer that you will make of us your own people, that health and healing, holiness and wholeness may mark our days, and be a blessing to all whom we meet. Amen.

Notes on use of this service, including dates, occasions and possible changes.

Mary, Model Mother

Call

Unless the Lord build the house, they labour in vain who build it; Unless the Lord watch the city, the watchman's work is in vain.

Prayer

Our God, we know you in your gifts, and in your loving tender care. In this time of worship may your spirit work in us to make us sensitive, caring, firm and tender, as we have seen your parenting to be. Through Christ we pray, Amen.

Scripture Reading

Luke 1:26-31; 2:13-19; 2:25-35

Suggested Hymns

29,   420 It would be most appropriate if a soloist could sing *Ave Maria*

Probably no subject has been painted or sculpted more often than Mary, mother of Jesus. It is striking in a gallery to come upon the traditional representation of her as the mother with the babe in her ams and then see beside it a "pieta", the grieving mother with her son in her arms once more.

From birth to death, from first to last, - faithful.

It is good to remind ourselves that the words, "Hail, Mary, blessed art thou among women ..." are not the invention or even the property of any one church. They are the words of the Bible and belong to all Christians. They can have particular meaning for us in the week of Mother's Day, Christian Family Sun-

day. The Holy Mother is a model of motherhood for all who take the faith seriously. Four phrases from the New Testament help us form a picture of Mary's mothering.

1) "And a sword shall pierce thy heart also". Mary and Joseph had brought the infant for dedication. The old priest who performed the ceremony was given a glimpse of future glory. He then turned to Mary with those shattering words. Recall those two mother-figures again - the child mother with her baby - the mourning mother with her son, lifeless, across her knees.

The Madonna of the Tear was painted 100 years ago by German artist, Hermann Kaulbach. His Mary is a very young, dark, Jewish girl, with haunting beauty, holding a fat, curly -headed, dark-skinned little boy. She has his hand to her lips and a tear is starting down her cheek. New mother, young wife, she is lonely and fearful, and it was only the beginning. Behind her, the search for a birthing place, the hurried preparation, and a delivery miles from home and the women she trusted. Ahead, she dimly senses a dizzying pace of events that will sweep her child to an early death. No wonder she is often referred to as Our Lady of Sorrows! "Blessed are you among women". There are many bruises on the road to such blessedness.

Yet mothers still wince with the pain the world inflicts on their children. An infant requires heart surgery, a young child is found to have cancer, a youngster is ridiculed at shool , a daughter marries a fellow whom parents are certain will bring her unhappiness. A mother wipes away the nosebleed that marks her child's first encounter with anger and pain and tries to explain why anyone would not like him. There is much talk of the joys of parenthood. The heartbreak is often ignored.

Mothers still find their resource for dealing with the pain where Mary did - in prayer, and the assurance of God's care. Such assurance allows mothers to reverse the old saying. "Don't do something; just stand there." And care.

2) "He was subject unto them". Parents have two tasks. One, to bring a child to birth. Two, to bring that child to personhood. The influence of his parent's home life is quite clear in the way that Jesus used it to illustrate everything he taught. A turn of the century hymn goes, "Faith of our mothers, guiding faith,/ For youthful longing, youthful doubts,/ How blurred our vision, blind our way,/ Thy providential care without./ Faith of our mothers, guiding faith, we will be true ...."

3) "Mary kept all these things, pondering them in her heart". Jesus must have been a source of bewilderment for his widowed mother. There was a rebel strangeness in the boy, the way he made rude comments on prominent leaders in the community. His boldness and his clashes with authority were not at first understood by her or his brothers and sisters. Yet she loved and accepted him throughout. In time she came to be a follower of her own son, but only after much tension within herself and in the family.

How hard it is for us to accept the difference between our children and ourselves. Yet each must find and follow his or her own style. We can provide ideals but not ambitions.

4) "Mary prayed with the apostles". This is the last the Bible has to say of her. It is not easy for parents to be parented by their children, but Mary models even that behavior. In his Jesus of Nazareth Kahlil Gibran has Mary say, at the end, "Behold, he who once lay against my heart is now throbbing in space." He adds, "and she was a woman fulfilled". May there come for each mother the day when she can say, "My soul doth magnify the Lord. And my spirit rejoices in God my Saviour."

Prayer
Of all our life's activities, O God, it is easist to fail as parents. Ouor own desires are so mixed with our hopes for our children that often we cannot sort out which belongs to whom. It is so easy to dismiss the needs of our children, for familiarity dulls our sensitivity. The frustrations of parenting makes us short and we miss the blessings of their presence until they are gone and we would wish them back. Keep us awake to the joys ofparenting , O you who are parent of us all. Amen.

Notes on use of this service, including dates, occasions and possible changes.

Wind and Fire

Call

And it shall come to pass, the Lord said,
that I will pour out my spirit on all flesh;
your sons and your daughters shall
prophesy, your old people shall dream
dreams, and your young people shall see
visions.
Come Holy Spirit, come.
Come as the fire and burn; come as the
wind and cleanse;
Come as the light and reveal.
Convict, convert, consecrate.
Come, Holy Spirit, come. Amen

Scripture Reading
Acts 2:1-13   Galatians 5:22-26

Suggested Hymns
379,   265

Happy Pentecost!
Now, what kind of greeting is that?
We've heard and repeated a number of
different greetings over the past few
months - Merry Christmas, Happy New
Year, Happy Easter, maybe Happy
Birthday or Happy Anniversary. So why
not Happy Pentecost?

Pentecost is the most exuberant of
Christian celebrations. Its earliest cele-
brants were accused of drinking new
wine and early on a working morning at
that! It might resemble the Heuringer of
Austria where the new wine is greeted
with nights of moonlit music, dancing
friends, rich food and gentle kisses.
Even with these incentives we are not
likely to get far in selling "Happy Pentecost" as an annual greeting.

Pentecost celebrates the coming of
God's holy spirit. Even that seems to
elicit little enthusiasm. Bishop Robinson, shocked the church world a few
years ago with his book, *Honest to God,*
which expressed more doubts and raised
more questions than most people
wanted to hear from a Bishop. In it he
said, *"The Holy Spirit is supremely the
'unknown God', the God-shaped blank
of our day ... the very word 'Ghost' used
of the spirit tells the tale. He is a phan-
tom: people simply don't know what
we're talking about"*

One might agree if the Bishop means
people are not familiar with the term, the
name. Not if he means they are unfamil-
iar with the experience. A theologian of
a century ago writes, "When the Holy
Ghost departs from any set of opinions
or form of character, they whither like a
sapless tree."

You may have noticed in the opening
prayer that the spirit is spoken of as wind
and fire. These are two of numerous
terms used to describe the spirit's activity. We err when we try to say how the
spirit must work. But we have observed
the spirit at work at these two ends of a
spectrum of activity.

There is a dramatic and fiery way of the
spirit. Fire sets on fire. Certainly the
spirit is contagious.

A great preacher of the last century,
often described as a man of fire, was
Phillips Broooks. As a young man he
showed no special promise. He trained

as a teacher but it was disastrous. He was fired by a principal who told him, "A man who cannot teach is good for nothing else."

Humiliated and dejected he talked to the President of Harvard, where he had graduated. He recommended that Brooks consider the ministry. As a young man Brooks had refused to be confirmed and had rarely been in church since. Still he did agree to attend seminary. One professor there talked of a personal relationship with the living Christ and of new life in the spirit in such a way that Brooks caught fire. When he graduated Churches were transformed by his leadership and while still a young man he went to famous Trinity Church in Boston where he had one of the most illustrious ministries imaginable. A business man said, "I don't know the answers to all my questions but when Phillips Brooks walks down the street I believe in God". Years later a man who as a youngster had heard Brooks preach could recall only one sentence yet that one had been a touchstone. "Flame leaps to flame." It did with Brooks.

The spirit comes also as wind, as breathe, the breathe of life. The spirit is as natural and gentle as air that gives us life without our knowing it.

Wherever one acts in mercy and love, the spirit is there, though unnamed. The Good Samaritan was acting in the spirit though he would never even have called himself "good", just a Samaritan doing his job.

Where there is joy, the spirit is present. In Updike's The Centaur a devout man whose son is offended by the ribald laughter that spills from a pub, checks

the boy with, "All joy belongs to the Lord".

When we feel gratitude, it is the work of the spirit. It must be agonizing for an atheist when he or she feels grateful. Who does she thank?

The artist reaching out after beauty, the scientist after truth, the reformer after goodness, all are empowered by the spirit though they may not name the name.

Whenever we feel a hollow place in our own lives - "try to remember, without a hurt the heart is hollow," - the spirit is at work, like the gentle wind. Phillips Brooks wrote to a young clergyperson, "Less and less grows the consciousness of seeking God. Greater and greater grows the certainty that God is seeking us and giving Himself to us to complete the measure of our capacities."

Prayer
Come as the fire, O Spirit, and burn, come as the wind and cleanse. Come, Holy Spirit, come. Amen.

Notes on use of this service, including dates, occasions and possible changes.

Enough Already

Call

Call

The writer of Proverbs says, "The plans of the mind belong to man, but the answer of the tongue is from the Lord. All the ways of a man are pure in his own eyes, but the Lord weighs the spirit."

Prayer

Almighty God, the unfolding year brings new beauty and strength with each passing week. We thank you now for the gifts of this season. Warm winds and May flowers bring us a rush of joy. The sun brings the promise of new growth in the world around us. May we also know inner growth as summer activities stretch our bodies, new ideas stretch our minds, and fresh encounters stretch our spirits. We ask all this in Jesus' Name. Amen.

Scripture Reading

Matthew 5:13-20

Suggested Hymns

281, 147

One way or another Elvis Presley stays in the news despite passing from the scene so long ago. Some who lived when he did will remember the swivelling hips as he sang, "I want to be free-ee-ee-ee." His sentiment flowered into a massive social movement that spurned all limits set, all lines drawn, all standards demanded. All in the name of the developing of persons.

The Christian faith has always had a place for "limits". It has claimed, in fact, that limits are necessary for freedom. In a recent seminar on drug abuse, a personable street worker said, "The time comes when you just have to say, 'Enough already'".

Out of Africa, a truly memorable film, swept the Academy Awards in 1986 From one viewpoint it was a study in freedom. In a telling episode Meryl Streep as Karen Blixen, and Robert Redford as Denys Finch-Hatton discuss Redford's unwillingess to accept any limitations on his behaviour.

He claims, "I don't want to find out one day that I'm at the end of someone else's life. I'm willing to pay for my freedom -to be lonely, to die alone if I have to. I think that's fair."

Streep's reply is fascinating. "Not quite. You want me to pay for your freedom. I am not allowed to need you, or rely on you, or expect anything of you. In the world you would make there would be no love at all."

Redford tries once more to justify himself. "There would be the best kind. The kind we wouldn't have to prove."

"You'd be living on the moon then. I have learned a thing you haven't. There are some things worth having. But they come with a price. I used to think you wanted nothing. Now I realize I was wrong. You want it all."

There is enough in that dialogue for a full evening's discussion. The theme is freedom - and its cost. Freeedom isn't free. We have had enough of the society fashioned to Finch-Hatton's desires.

Jesus was rarely *judgemental* but notice how often he used *limiting* terms. "It has been said to you ... but I say to you..." Notice, too,that this phrase occurs just after the beatitudes which, in themselves, advocate some pretty strict limitations on the self-seeking of the Christian. Its hard to be humble, merciful, pure, peacemaking, without imposing healthy limits on one's self-aggrandisment. What was once seen as a restriction can be seen through Jesus' eyes as a "channeling".

It was thought at one time that if we were to remove all restrictions and inhibitions the result would be a healthier and happier people. The rebellion of the 60's and the Me-Seeking self-centeredness of the 70's has, instead, brouoght an increasing incidence of depression and alienation. One psychiatrist says we have shifted from Freud's "Guilty Man" to today's "Tragic Man".

Maxine Schnall. in the 60's, hosted a hotline radio show that extolled the wonders of living with no limits. Now she has written a best-seller, *Limits*, in which she writes, *"In pursuing liberation without any understanding of the need for limits we wound up with less freedom than we had before."*

In a large Canadian city a family from a wealthy area were told about a huge bargain food outlet where they could buy groceries for much less than in their own neighbourhood. They drove their station wagon down to the food terminal. The customers weren't quite their kind of people, but the price was right. They loaded up with cases of canned good and produce. On the way home the axel broke. Sounds rather like one of Jesus' parables updated.

From the first chapter of Genesis where our mythical parents testing the boundaries, throughout human history, and in our day we have found that it is at the boundaries we meet the presence of God - first as Judge, then as Redeemer, then as Teacher. In this is our hope for renewal and a life that is not "on the moon" but as good as it can be upon earth.

Prayer

Our God, you have given us so much with your gift of life, yet we wish always for more. We push beyond the boundaries. May we be aware of how that striving creates burdens for those around us. We would pray for all who bear sorrows unseen yet heavy on the heart, those who feel an inner shame that needs the cleansing of your love and ours. Those who are exploited for the satisfaction of others, especially those whom they love. So may our prayers and reflections not be casual this day, but standing in the deep center of our own needs grant us grace to stretch out hands of care to others in Jesus' name. Amen.

Notes on use of this service, including dates, occasions and possible changes.

A Tourist in Your Own Hometown

Call

The Psalmists cries out, "Awake, my soul. Awake, O harp and lyre. I will awake the dawn. I will give thanks to thee, O lord God. I will sing and make melody. For your steadfast love is great above the heavens and your faithfulness reaches to the clouds.

Prayer

God, bless us we pray, as we meet for worship. Bless us with the gift of awareness - to have eyes - and see; to have ears - and hear; to have the gift of touch - and to feel. These we would know - now. Bring to brighter flame our love for you that it may be both radiant and constant, through Christ our Lord. Amen.

Scripture Reading

Mark 9:33-37; 42-50   10:13-16

Suggested Hymns

129,   19

Unless you become as a little child, you shall not enter the Kingdom of Heaven - you shall not know that the Kingdom of Heaven is all around you now.

The child takes nothing for granted. All life is fresh and marvellous. The child-like spirit is personified in Zorba the Greek, in the novel, on stage, in the film.

Zorba's "Boss" says of him, "I felt as I listened to Zorba that the earth was recovering its pristine freshness. All the dulled daily things regained the brightness they had in the beginning , when they came from the hand of God. Water,
women, the stars, bread, returned to their mysterious primitive origin, and the divine whirlwind burst once more upon the air."

What a fine attitude with which to approach the summer months - days of beauty, times of leisure.

Look at your own neighbourhood with the eyes of a child. A neighbourhood of fine old houses can overwhelm the senses. Sometimes it helps to focus. With your hands on either side of your face, you frame each building, as the viewfinder on a camera does, concentrating on each house and garden individually The full impress of each structure will then occur. It is a process of "centering".

Ernest Campbell, noted preacher, suggests that we enjoy our own town or city by "becoming a tourist in our own hometown", by acting as if we were seeing it all for the first time. That spirit can bring us to each summer day singing, "Morning has broken, like the first morning". See your own home as the gift that it is. As if for the first time, observe its colours and shapes and lines. It was one who took notice of the beauty around him who advised, "Consider the lilies..."

This summer watch people with the eyes of a child. How often it is said of Jesus that he "beheld" - the woman, the man, the child! His gaze would rest on that person, taking her out of the multitude and restoring her to personhood. Individuals lost in the crowd regained individuality in Jesus caring look.

We so easily slip into identifying people by their function or appearance- a cop, a clerk, a punker,a "doll". This summer step back a bit and look beyond the garb, the surface appearance. Look beyond the face and into the heart. The more relaxed pace of summer allows it. Ask God for a fresh appreciation of the place you live and the people you live with. See Jesus, this summer, through the eyes of a child. Ian Burnett, a past great Presbyterian preacher in Ottawa talked of "Faithless familiarity" saying, "the fact is that Jesus of Nazareth is as familiar to most of us as our own shadows; but the tragedy is, he is no more real." A summer of reading and meditation could yield the kind of exciting encounter with the Man from Nazareth that the disciples had. The summer can be a mellow time of "meeting" for the Spirit.

Prayer

As our minds reach forward towards the summer months, O God, we are aware of brothers and sisters for whom this season brings no joy. We think of those who live where sunlight cannot penetrate the barrier of buildings, nor brighten the narrow cluttered streets; where, when the light does fall it reveals garbage and grime and brings heat but no warmth. We think of homes that are beautiful to see but where lives are drab and lonely. We think of families who come to vacation time with spirits crippled by death or desertion or divorce. We pray for a world where family feelings break down into hostility and hatred. We have thought together of how our spirits might be lifted in these summer months. Help us to practise the skills of the spirit

that will deepen our appreciation for all that you have given.

We would thank you, O God, for June days, for closing events and graduations, for farewells and vacation plans. We belive that with each ending you open up the prospect of new beginnings. May our plans for the summer months include time for you and an openess to your leading. Amen.

Notes on use of this service, including dates, occasions and possible changes.

Cords of Love

Call

Let us know the Lord. Let us press on to know the Lord. For his going forth is as sure as the dawn; he will come to us as the showers, as the spring rains that water the earth.

Prayer

Lord God, Maker of all things, you who did look on all creation and see that it was good, we thank you for the love with which you have followed us to this day. We thank you for the gift of life that stirs us to work and to pleasure; for the good earth, our home, for friends, and community, but especially this day we are grateful for for families. We thank you for the parents who nurtured us and guided us, for children who challenge us and change us, for grandchildren who enliven us and open for us once again horizons we might easily ignore, for nieces and nephews who broaden our family circle. Greater than all of these, O God, is our wonder at your own love. Yours, O God, is the love of a good parent binding us to life with the confidence that comes to children learning in the shadow of a loving father and mother. For this assurance we give you thanks in the name of Jesus , our elder brother, Amen.

Scripture Reading

Hosea ll (not easy reading, try to find time to rehearse beforehand).

Suggested Hymns

134, 198 (suggested alternative tune).

Hosea the prophet lived an obscure and sad life 800 years before the birth of Jesus and left just a few pages of his preaching as a legacy. Even these came to the editors in bits and pieces so that their best efforts resulted in no more than a garbled and disjointed little book of the Bible. Yet it was apparently a favorite of Jesus. He quoted from it more often than from any other book in his own scriptures.

Hosea's tenderness and sympathy resulted in the most compassionate picture of God to be found in the Old Testament. God is depicted as a loving marriage partner and as a good parent.

The prophet's insight grew out of his private tragedy. His wife, to whom he was devoted, was unfaithful. He was not certain their children were his. She became a prostitute and then a slave. Hosea, it seems, after their marriage and her subsequent slavery, purchased her and took her home as a guest in his home. In his mind he fused his experience with that of Jehovah. God, too, had been deserted - by his people. Yet he could not give up on his love for them. Hosea saw God struggling, just as he had, between vengeful anger and yearning love. It was a bold analogy, yet Jesus seems to have blessed it by his fascination with the book.

Hosea saw God as a parent who at the beginning lifted and carried his people and then in time taught them to walk. Like a human parent, God cares for us from helplessness to independence. Yet even when the child has become an adult and walks unaided the family ties remain. Hosea speaks of them as bonds of compassion, cords of love. He speaks of reins and harness. We continue something of the same feling in our term "family bonds".

All these are means of guidance. They are not meant to coerce or intimidate but to give direction. They are so light as to be invisible, yet they are strong. They secure without smothering. What are these "cords of comapssion" in our own family life?

Hosea saw in God a capacity for listening. Over and over he spoke of God as one who listened to the pleas of his people. "Listening" is one of the cords of compassion. Listening is to be distinguished from merely waiting our turn to talk. True listening is an active, strenuous, and ultimately exhausting exercise. True listening draws life from the other. Probably no figure in history illustrates this gift as well as Jesus does. Let your mind go to the many conversations in the New Testament where Jesus helped others to recognize their own possibilities simply by listening to them. As the body thrives on exercise, nutrition and sleep, so the spirit thrives on love and listening.

It is evident that Hosea, as a single parent, must have done some discussing, too. Parents talk even to the newborn who can comprehend nothing. In good parenting, conversation, the other side of listening, continues through all life. With all the disruption of family life that his children knew, it was essential that Hosea keep all avenues of communication open. His teen-age boys must haved appreciated knowing that they were free to talk, to sort out their feelings

and their decisions with a parent who would both listen and counsel.

Family rituals are another one of many cords of compassion that bind the family together. Family vacations, festive occasions, naming the pets, family council. These make memories at a time when we probably have no idea how important those memories will be. By these and many more ties the family is bound into a unit of love and learning as God intended it to be.

Prayer
Lord God of Hosea and of Jesus, of the solitary and of the family, bless our efforts to understand one another, and to join our lives with others in the growth that you purpose for us. For parents and for children, in a world of bewildering change, we pray. Keep us steady in the face of perplexity and competing interests. Grant us sensitivity to the needs of those around us and to your will for us. Amen.

Notes on use of this service, including dates, occasions and possible changes.

Ut Omnes Sint

Call

Jesus Christ came and preached peace to you who were far off and peace to those who were near; for through him we both have access in one Spirit to the Father.

Prayer

O God, the Creator of all humankind, who by your Holy Spirit has made a diversity of peoples one, in the confession of your name, lead us, we pray you, by the same spirit, to display to the whole earth one mind in belief and one passion for righteousness, through Christ our Lord. Amen.

Scripture Reading

Isaiah 6:1-9   John 17:6-26

Suggested Hymns

147,   146

In a study group at an international meeting, a young Japanese student whose English was excellent but whose pronunciation was less precise, kept talking about "Daminations". He was attempting to say, "denominations" but some felt that his pronunciation brought him close to the truth.

In God's providence, however, there was probably a time for denominations. They form a rich tapestry of thought and practise as one looks backwards through history. They provide also, unfortunately, excuses for bitterness and bloodshed.

John Grant, leading church historian, has written. "The emergence of denomi-

nations has brought good to the world and the church. It has meant an end to persecution. It has opened the way to the recognition that the life of faith flows in many different channels." "It has served a purpose."

The purpose of which he writes has been served only when we recognize the values, the gifts, that have been brought by our denominations.

The notion of denominations is a late one in history. The acceptance of one church divided into "churches" is a recent one. The church has existed for 2,000 years; denominations, as we think of them, for only 300. The one church did split almost 1,000 years after its origin. That division reflected the separation of east and west in the Mediterranean lands. In 1054 the eastern church, centered in Constantinople, claimed independence from the authority of the Bishop of Rome. Thus the *Orthodox* church came into being, familiar in the onion-shaped domes of Ukranian churches on the prairies and in major cities.

The reform that is closer to our own church life was the final result of a bubbling unrest that went on for 150 years, flaring up and dying down, until in 1517, Martin Luther's attempts at reform were accepted by large numbers of Christians. The reformers would each have been appalled at the thought of creating a separate church. For them there was and would always be one church. They certainly hoped that the one church would change - and each had suggestions about what changes should occur. They all looked for a more simple form of worship, a morally stringent lifestyle for all Christians, lay and cleric, an end to political alliances, and more flexibility in dealing with the spiritual needs of the people. Despite their hopes for unity the movement fragmented the one church into a dozen major denominations, and eventually into hundreds of minor ones.

Looking back over that long history, what gifts have come to us? The early church - the first 1,000 years, gave us the incredible bravery of the martyrs in Rome, missionary drive, the first solid statements of Christian experience in words, the monasteries that kept learning alive through the dark ages, and heroic leaders like Joan of Arc, Francis of Assissi and many more. This heritage Protestants and Roman Catholics share as a mutual legacy.

From the Reformed churches we have inherited simplicity and naturalness, a determination to get to the heart of the faith in personal terms. From the Lutherans - respect for scripture. From the Reformed church of Calvin, via Knox's Presbyterian version of it, scholarship and a deep sense of the majesty of God. From the Anglicans, a love of liturgy and history. From the Congregationalists, an independent spirit and the claims of civic responsibility. From the Baptists an insistence on personal committment. From the Methodists, social concern and a love of song. From the many denominations of the Holiness Movement, joy and spontaneity.

We are grateful for this rich tapestry. It belongs to us all. Now the time has come for it to flow back together. John Grant, who wrote of the gifts brought by denominations also wrote, "now they must go." Their purpose served, they must now whither. The movement to reunion, - the ecumenical movement - is for many the most thrilling feature of church life in our century. "Is Christ divided?" Paul protested. Those who have had the rich and powerful experience of attending an international meeting of world churches are glad to answer Paul - "the divisions are healing! Christ will be divided no longer." No gift from the denominations need be lost, but Christ's prayer that "all may be one" - ut omnes sint - is being answered by our choice and by a powerful movement of God's spirit.

Prayer

(from the Vancouver Assembly of the World Council of Churches 1983) O God, we thank you for the wholeness of the human family; for the rich variety of human experience and the gifts we bring to one another when we meet in a spirit of acceptance and love. For all that comes from mutual enrichment and growing understanding we are grateful, Amen.

Notes on use of this service, including dates, occasions and possible changes.

Barnabas

Call

O sing, O sing joyfully unto the Lord, our strength. Make a cheerful sound, make a cheerful sound unto the God of Jacob.

Prayer

O Lord God, all the earth worships you. They sing praises to you, they sing praises to your name. You cover the earth with clouds, you prepare the rain for the earth, you make grass to grow upon the hills. You give all things their life. So we praise you with heart and voice, now and forever. Amen.

Scripture Reading

Acts 4:32-37; 9:26-28; 11:19-26.

Suggested Hymns

374 (suggested alternate tune 216) 299

The Bible is an old book, full of old history and old stories, yet it is not old-fashioned. In today's scripture we meet one of the most up-to-date persons imaginable.

Barnabas, the Bible tells us, was a kindly man, full of the Holy Spirit, and of strong faith. He is a man worthy of attention.

His real name was Joseph. Nicknames bore great significance for the New Testament church. They were given, almost as medals of honour, to distinguish a person and his or her outstanding characteristics. So the new name often had an important meaning. Barnabas was such a nickname.

One of the strongest names one could devise, Barnabas means "Son of Encouragement". It is true to the nature of the man. Each time we encounter Barnabas in the New Testament he is assisting someone else, often Paul, to be his or her best . The earliest mention of Barnabas is at the time when the church is becoming a true commune - each is giving all, that it may serve the needs of the whole. In this very tense situation, by a generous and gallant gesture, Barnabas gave a strong lead that got the project off to a good start. (It is natural that he would become the patron saint of "giving"). In every mention of him we find a strong, virile, caring person.

This is nowhere more evident than in his dealings with Paul. When Paul returned to Jerusalem from his trip to Damascus and his conversion on the way, a very ticklish scene developed. A powerful persecutor of the Christians, Paul had been converted on the Damascus Road, but the news had not yet reached the Christians in Jerusalem. They had only his word and that was not enough for many, especially for those whose families who had suffered under his orders. Only Barnabas had the insight, the faith and the courage to see the possibilities in this man, and to gamble by standing surity for him. By his generous spirit Barnabas turned Christian history inside out, opening the door for the most influential Christian thinker of all time.

When it seemed that the Gentiles were ready to hear the good news, it required a person of good sense, yet full of the

Holy Spirit, to make a judgement about whether this was really the right move for the church. Barnabas was the obvious choice.

The result of his inquiry was that he dedicated his life to telling the good news to the Gentiles. It was more than one person could do. His mind went immediatly to his friend, Paul.

Barnabas was a big man, in every way. His powerful build marked him for leadership and, as the two took off to spread the story of Christ, it was Barnabas who took the lead, with wiry little Paul trotting beside him. In one rural area they were mistaken for Zeus and Mercury!

The story contains one of those subtle nuances that tell a great deal about the persons involved. Luke, the writer of Acts, almost unconsciously, it seems, stops referring to Barnabas and Paul and starts writing of Paul and Barnabas. The leadership has quietly shifted, as it was bound to do. Yet it takes a big person to let such a change occur without protest. Barnabas easily stepped aside for the person he had himself sponsored. The mentor takes over from the cheif, and the chief is joyously willing.

Unfortunately the relationship had a sad ending. John Mark, young nephew to Barnabas, had accompanied them on their first missionary voyage, but he had become homesick and returned home. As they planned for their second trip Barnabas wanted to give young John Mark a second chance. Paul, also true to form, had refused. The two had quarreled and parted. Barnabas soon afterwards left with his nephew, but before they had gone far Barnabas was assasinated.

What a wasted life! Yet when we discover what happened to John Mark we realize that "encouragement" will win out. Of all the books of the Bible it is safe to say that the four gospels are the most frequently read. One was written by a young man who once faltered and failed, and could have been lost, but was encouraged, given a second chance and went on to become St. Mark. What's more, decades later, when Paul, as an old man, was led out to the Appian Way to be beheaded, one man stood with him to put an encouraging arm round his shoulder as he knelt - John Mark - kept by encouragement.

Prayer
Lord God, we know of your encouraging love. You have made us and raised us, held us and directed us, lifted us and set us on our feet again. May each of us in our own ways reach out an encouraging hand to others through Christ our Lord. Amen

Notes on use of this service, including dates, occasions and possible changes.

Jesus Wept

Call

Let us go into the house of the Lord. Our feet shall stand within thy gates, O Jerusalem. For my families and my companions sake I will say, "Peace be within your gates".

Prayer

Lord God, you have shaped our human history and even now you hold the universe in your care like a mother holds a child. Hear our prayer and bring us both the comfort and the challenge that is the gift of good parenthood, through him who was your child and has become our Master. Amen.

Scripture Reading

John ll:32-35 Luke 19:28, 36-42.

Suggested Hymns

72, 38 (suggested alternate tune 155).

Jesus wept. The shortest verse in the Bible.

Those who travel to Israel and walk where the disciples walked are often moved deeply by one shrine. It is a small Franciscan chapel on the Mount of Olives, overlooking the city of Jerusalem. It is in the shape of a tear-drop and is called the church of Dominus Flavut - the church of our Lord's tears.

It is in this spot that Jesus is said to have stood looking out across the city as he made his last entrance on Palm Sunday. That city which had been the center of his people's hopes for generations,stood there rich and golden in the sunlight. Jesus looked and the futility of his hopes caught at his throat. "Oh Jerusalem, Jerusalem, how often would I have taken you under my wings as a hen her chicks, but you would not". And Jesus wept.

It was not the first time scripture had recorded Jesus' tears. Just on the other side of the high hill that North Americans find difficult to call a "Mount" lies the city of Bethany. Bethany had been a second home to Jesus. While in Jerusalem, the sophisticated and crowded city, so different to his country home in Nazareth, he had found shelter with good friends in Bethany, Lazareth and his sisters, Mary and Martha.

In the last week of his life, the week of his tears over Jerusalem, Jesus walked back over that hill each night to stay in friendly Bethany. Just a few months earlier Bethany had been the scene of one of the most dramatic acts of his ministry. Lazareth, his friend, had been ill. Jesus, in Jerusalem, received word, but did not leave for Bethany until too late. When he arrived Lazarus was dead. Mary spoke to him in a tone that is hard to imagine in addressing the Christ. Accusingly she said, "If only you had been here this would not have happened!"

His reply wil never be forgotten. "I am the resurrection and the life. Whosoever lives and believes in me shall never die."

Why Jesus was so long in coming is a

mystery, especially wnen he seemed always so responsive to need. There is no puzzle about his feelings though. At the tomb, Jesus wept. Some feel that tears are unworthy of a grown man. Others will claim that they are certainly unworthy of a Messiah.

Something important is being said in this story - about Jesus, and about us.

There is an old Jewish saying, "What soap is for the body, tears are for the soul." And Charles Dickens' Mr. Bumble says it well, "Weeping is good for us. It opens the lungs, washes the countenance, exercises the eyes, and softens the temper." Tears are cleansing, refreshing, empowering - and natural!

Jesus' tears, on either side of the mountain are of two sorts. On the Bethany side he sheds tears of personal pain and grief. On the Jerusalem side it is the sorrow of the world that brings tears to his eyes.

Each is a genuine form of mourning, the kind of mourning of which Jesus spoke much earlier in his minstry. "Blessed are you who mourn for you shall be comforted." The German reads "Blessed are the leidtragen ", the bearers of sorrows, those who carry in their hearts the sorrows of the world.

Jesus marked these people as special because they were willing to risk their feelings as Jesus was. He wept - in full public view. Strength, competence, sucess, are all real. But so are despair, fear, and failure. Real life comes when we live intimately with agony and ecstasy, with pain and pleasure, with tears and laughter. It is clear that this is Jesus' way.

Prayer

Our God, even in our own homes and in our own lives, we feel at times that we are strangers in a strange land. Familiar faces and natural actions seem out of place, for we are assailed by failure, and sorrow. Some have experienced betrayal and desertion and others feel lost within themselves. We, too have hung our harps on the willows and felt the songs stop in our throats. So we ask your presence and with it your blesssed gifts of patience, and courage and perserverance. We rejoice in the knowledge that Jesus walked this way, tasted the salt of his own tears, yet walked on to triumph. So would we in his name. Amen.

Notes on use of this service, including dates, occasions and possible changes.

What's So Funny

Many of us were taught, by example if not in word, that there was no place for laughter in church. A few years ago the late Willis Wheatley produced for the United Church a series of pen sketches of the face of Jesus. Most were well received but one drew fire. It showed Jesus with his head back roaring with laughter. "Surely", people wrote, "Jesus never laughed aloud like that". A wry smile perhaps, but no belly laughs. Who knows, but his tales indicate a grand sense of humour, like the fellow removing a speck from a friend's eye when he can hardly see for the chunk of bark in his own.

The story of Sarah is riddled with humour. In some ways the whole Abraham and Sarah story is a comedy of errors. A successful businessman in a sophisti-cated and cultured corner of the ancient world gives up everything because God has spoken to him in a dream. Just imagine how he explained that to his business buddies in the coffee shop in Ur! What's more the messsage was that God would bless the whole world through the descendants of this couple. What descendants? The couple had no children and Sarah was well past the age of conception.

Still they obeyed. With a huge retinue they made their way out of the lush fertile valley of the Euphrates, across desert land westward to the so-called "Promised Land" - a barren and rocky wilderness inhabited by hostile native peoples. After some misadventures in Egypt they finally reached their destination and settled in but a family squabble resulted in the other side of the family getting the green valleys of the Jordan, and Abraham and Sarah getting the West Bank.

Still the story continued. As one preacher wrote, "The years rolled by like empty perambulators" until an angel arrived to say that God was going to make good his promise. Sarah, at 90 years, was going to have a baby! One account tells us that Abraham fell on his face laughing, another that Sarah, hiding behind the tent door, began to giggle and got them all going, perhaps even the angel. There was lusty laughter out on the plains that day. Suddenly God intervened and asked why Sarah laughed. The point is that God is not angry. Rather, God blesses their laughter and tells them that the child's name shall be Isaac - which means "Laughter".

Matthew Fox, popular Domincan author, contrasts "Sarah's Circle" with Jacob's ladder. Rather than Jacob's straight on linear and competitive approach, Sarah adopts a dancing, laughter-filled lifestyle that has in it a creativity that is symbolized in her laughter.

It is as important to look at the laughter of Sarah and Jesus as it is to look at their tears. Laughter punctures the pomposity of self-important people. Jesus used it for that purpose often. There were probably residents of Nazareth who resented having their foolish foibles turn up in his stories. Much of the laughter in the New Testament is akin to that of cartoons in which loveable kids knocks hats off overly dignified gentlemen, reducing them to a more mortal level.

Comedy has us look through the wrong end of the telescope till we laugh at our own littleness. In his play *A Thousand Clowns* Herb Gardner says of a young character. *"He sees street jokes. He sees subway farce and cross-town bus humour and all the cartoons people make by being alive. "* Exactly the kind of humour that Jesus displays.

On a more positive level, laughter hallows hope. Abraham and Sarah had seen about as much grimness in life as anyone, yet we hear the unexpected sound of laughter and see the tent shake with it. It reminds us of an old saying, "Laughter is God's hand on the shoulder of a troubled world."

Human life inevitably holds disappoint-

ment and discouragement, suffering and sorrow, but our God is not only the God of the inevitable but also the God of the unexpected and unpredictable. He is the God of the prepostrous and the hilarious, and with him nothing is impossible.

In the *Divine Comedy*, Dante making his final ascent to heaven, hears the choir of angels singing the praises of Almighty God, and says, "And it seemed like the laughter of heaven."

Prayer
Out of the whirling matter that was before time began you have fashioned our universe, O God. In the vast sweep of space you touched this tiny planet into life, the life of green growth and whispering winds, the life of human love and laughter,the life of mind and spirit. We are grateful heirs of your creative power, and wisdom and care. So we rejoice in the dependable cycle of seasons - the wonder of green grass and bright flowers,the wonder of a newborn's cry, a baby's throaty chuckle, of parent's pride and grandparent's joy. Above all we are grateful for Jesus, whose words and way make sense of it all. In his name we pray. Amen.

Notes on use of this service, including dates, occasions and possible changes.

Blessed is the Nation

Call

Unless the Lord build the house, they labour in vain who build it. Unless the Lord watch over the city, the watchman stays awake in vain.

Prayer

Almighty God, who has called us out of many nations, and set our feet in this broad land, establishing us as one people from sea to sea; we remember, with gratitude, the way that you have led us to this time. Grant us through this time of worship and praise, a new appreciation for the beauty and wonder of our land, that we may magnify your name among all nations, serving you and your family, with joy, through Christ. Amen.

Scripture Reading

Romans 12:1-13

Suggested Hymns

216, 212 (suggested alternate tune 299)

Blessed is the nation whose God is the Lord. There has probably been no nation that has not at some point in its history felt itself to be favoured of God. Today we tend to be a bit more cynical about politics and even about patrtiotism. Still, when an Olympic gold medalist from Canada mounts the stand we feel a swell of pride as we hear our national anthem played.

About two-thirds of the Bible deals with the relationship between God and the nation. The whole of the Hebrew scriptures relates in one way or another the story of the destiny of Israel under God. The Old Testament represents almost two thousand years of reflection on God and the nation.

It would seem reasonable to expect that we are still called upon to consider the responsibility and destiny of the nation, in the light of God's will. Just as we think of the significance of our own lives when we come to a birthday, so whenever we come to our nation's birthdate we think of its life under God.

Three responses seem appropriate. First, we are grateful to the Lord of lands, for our own land. Some have been fortunate to live in several provinces. They may have experienced what Earl Birnie called "a slow smash in the eye with all that geography can utter" - his image of our westernmost province. Some think of the beauty of golden wheat swelling the great Canadian granary, or the simple beauty of the early crocus on the prairie. Other have come to love the throbbing heartland of our nation, where industry and commerce light up an unending skyline. Some have tapped toes at une nuit *folklorique* with soaring fiddles and tapping spoons. Still others have caught breath at the stunning highland scenery as mists have broken on the sea below the Cabot Trail, or over the tossing waters of Portugal Cove. When such joy and pride is felt, it is good to have a Giver to thank.

A second response is humility. "When I consider the works of your hands, what are we that you love us." A look at our land gives us the perspective we need for true humility, which is not to think little of ourselves, but to think much of God. The vastness of creation alongside the sweep of time, give us the viewpoint of the Psalmists who caugfht the spirit of true humility in countless memorable verses. "A thousand years in your sight" are like a moment in our time, like a watch in the night.

The third response is needed today. It is hope. A look back over our history as a nation shouild provide hope. Both francophone and anglophone Canadians have played games with the myth of the Plains of Abraham. No war was won on those heights. Two foreign armies, under leaders who detested the land where they were forced to fight, fouight a tough but minor battle in a war that was won and lost on the battlefields of Belgium. In the peace settlement afterwards, the British Parliament debated for many days on whether to return to France, Canada or Guadalupe. They decided to be generous, in hopes of a more amiable future, and gave up the prize - Guadalupe!!

Not long afterwards violent revolution rocked our continent, and insurrection left the land torn in half. Still the nation has survived and grown. Old emneties have healed and new alliances have brought fresh strength. A serious look at our history provides hope for the future.

Christian hope, however, has its roots in deeper soil. God speaks to national life through the words of Isaiah. "Listen to me, O coastlands, and hearken you people from afar - I will give you as a light to the nations, that my salvation shall reach the ends of the earth".

Here are all the possibilities of arrogant pride. Here also are the possibilities of the nation being a humble instrument in the hands of God. May each of us in our national life, in our political, economic,and family lives, be as willing to pioneer a new way of life as our ancestors were. We are called on, by God, to weld a new national identity, bringing together a diversity of peoples. That means openess, learning, flexibility and a willingness to risk giving up old ways in exhange for new. May God help us to meet the challenge.

Prayer
God of the nations, we are grateful that your love underlies all the histories of all peoples. You have made of one blood all the nations of the earth. May we enjoy and appreciate the heritage that is ours. May we also to appreciate the gifts that others nations bring to our world. Amen.

Notes on use of this service, including dates, occasions and possible changes.

Dealing with the Dry Times

Call

We can say with the Psalmist: O God, you are our God. Early will we seek you., Our souls thirst for you as in a dry and weary land where no water is.

And God will reply: I will open up fountains in the midst of the valleys, and shall make the wilderness a pool of water so the wilderness and the dry land shall be glad, and the desert shall rejoice and blossom as a rose.

Prayer

O Lord Jesus Christ,you humbled yourself to baptism and temptation. Grant that we may rejoice in our own baptism into a community of faith. May we be strengthened by it to meet all temptation with wisdom and grace even though the wilderness and the dry times threaten to parch the spirit within us. Be present with us in all seasons, O Lord. Amen.

Scripture Reading

Matthew 3:13-4:ll (It is suggested that different voices read the separate speeches of Jesus and the Tempter).

Suggested Hymns

433 (possible alternate tune 384)
272 (possible alternate tune 352)

Then Jesus was led by the Spirit into the wilderness.

And wilderness it was and still is! The visitor to Israel sees the lush green valley floor where the Jordan flows by Jericho and where Jesus was baptized. The toulrist then looks up into one of the most barren, stony, badlands imaginable. Desolate as a soul without hope, the Mount of Temptation, stands above the valley like a grim world all its own. For Jesus, it was the dry time in every way. For us, as for Jesus, the dry times will come. They may follow close on glory, as they did for Jesus, the classic "let down". They may arise from stress or anxiety when all adaptive energy is exhuasted, or they may simply catch us unawares with no reason or warning. But come they will.

We wonder ,"Is God real? If God is real,is he near? If God is near, then does God care?"

Christian history records a dry time for every true believer. The accumulated experience of the ages testifies that for the dry time the revival of the spirit can be generated by two things - 1) Stillness and quiet 2) the fellowship of understanding company.

First, "Be still and know that I am God."

Our culture tell us. "Don't dwell on it. Stay busy. Do things." Good advice for some forms of depression, but not for the dry time of the soul. This is a time for putting down roots even in the hard baked soil of the dry time.

It is not easy to reverse our North American activism. Yet healing comes with quietness, with expectant waiting, and with an understanding of the affliction. Those in the helping professions learn that there are times when the old adage must be reversed. "Don't just stand there, do something" we are told. But when it is the spirit that is in trauma we are often better to say, "Don't do something; just stand there."

Years ago, Harry Emerson Fosdick,wrote, "We cannot live in unrelieved din and confusion and still grow a soul."

God is. In the stillness we reach out to God confident that God reaches out to us. God is to be addressed, to be talked to not just talked about.

If we are unable to talk with God, then we let our minds move over the events of the past few weeks, looking for disclosures of God's nature, and care, and purpose, as one on vacation combs the beach for shells and stones in the tangle of seaweed and driftwood. We reflect on what we have seen and heard and experienced in our commonplace relationships and circumsances, alert for signs of God's presence. These reflections will provide occasions for confession, for thanksgiving, for request, for intercession, even for protest, perhaps.

This is a living relationship in which prayer can become as natural as conversation with a well-loved friend. It may mean resting in God or wrestling with God, but it will be real.

The second avenue out of the dry time is fellowship. Jesus said, "Where two or three are gathered in my name, there am I." Religion has been defined as "The flight of the alone to the alone". There certainly are times in the religious life when we are alone with God. So are there times when God expects to find us in company with others.

A fine man, dying of cancer, wrote to friends, on his last Christmas, "I have periods of discouragement, coloured by an inescapable sense of aloneness ... but after months of absence I took in the church's Christmas musical. In part, I went to collect on all the promises of hugs and kisses relayed to me by Kay over the fall - and left few outstanding!! What a circle of great friends ..."

It is no accident that the mood changes as he writes of friends. It seems to be the intention of God that friendship is a soil in which the spirit grows. Friendship nourishes the spirit as food nourishes the body and learning the mind.

Prayer
There are days even months, O God, when prayer dies on our lips. Then we ask that your spirit pray through us for we know that you are the hunger as well as the bread. Amen.

Notes on use of this service, including dates, occasions and possible changes.

Philemon

Call
Jesus said, "You shall know the truth and the truth shall make you free." In word and song, in asking and in listening, we seek God's truth and freedom.

Prayer
Almighty God, to whom all thoughts are open and from whom no secrets are hid, cleanse the thoughts of our hearts by the inspiration of your Holy Spirit, that we may worthily magnify your glorious name, now and forever. Amen.

Scripture Reading
the Book of Philemon (It would be best if everyone had a Bible and read over the letter as it is read aloud by the leader)

Suggested Hymns
147, 242

The sun is rising over the towering columns of classic Rome. In the early shadows of the day two men are standing just outside the heavy walls of a city prison. A guard stands near by. The two are lost in conversation for a time, then the older man puts his arm around the shoulder of the younger. Their heads bow in prayer. The young man walks quickly away, out of the city walls and northward into the hills.

In the young man's wallet is a letter.

That letter, you have just read. It was addressed to the third person in a fascinating trio. These three men would have been judged unlikely candidates to alter the course of history, yet they did so.

One was a short, tough, travelling evanglist; the second a successful businessman in an obscure town in an outback of the Roman empire; and the third a slave - a runaway slave at that!

It was strange that the three should ever have met at all. It happened in the small town of Collosae on the Meander river about a 100 miles from Ephesus, the capital of the area, in what would now be called Turkey.

The evangelist will be quickly recognized as the apostle Paul. The letter was addressed to the businessman, Philemon, and it dealt with the fate of the young man who carried it, the runaway slave, Onesimus. Paul had met Philemon on one of his missionary voyages, and had probably met Onesimus at the same time. When the slave escaped and made his way to Rome, he somehow encountered Paul once more, and as so often happened when people met Paul, they also met Paul's master, Jesus. Onesimus became a Christian. He moved into prison with Paul and acted as his servant there.

Now Paul had a dillemma. He could not keep a runaway slave indefinitely, yet he was familar with the normal punishment for runaways -a branding iron, that would mark him forever. A runaway slave could even be executed if his master chose that. Onesimus must return. He returned carrying one of the most revolutionary letters ever written. The letter contained formal greetings, some friendly banter, even a pun on the name Onesiumus which, literally, means "useful". Paul noted that Onesimus had been "useful" to him! It is the most personal of Paul's letters.

Paul did not say to give Onesimus his freedom. He did not condemn the institution of slavery. That would be asking too much.

Paul said, simply, Onesimus is your brother in Christ. That is all that needed be said. The slaveowner must then work out what that meant for him. "He is your brother for whom Christ died." Those words ultimately destroy all rank, caste, hierarchy, class. All superior-subordinate relationships disappear. In writing this letter, which would in time find its way into the Bible, Paul undermined slavery and began a movement that would eventually lead to the enshrining of human rights into the constitution of nation after nation. The conviction that underlay this little letter was the seed that finally split the rock.

In the eyes of those who spoke Greek a slave was not even a person. The word for slave was anthropon - one who resembles a man. BUT IS NOT. He can be treated as a dog because his life is precisely equal to a dog's.

But all that is far in the past! Or is it! A film was released in 1987, *The Wansee Conference.* It simulates an 85 minute conference held in a Berlin suburb in 1941. The topic on the agenda of a group representing the Nazi bureaucracy, the SS, and the Gestapo was the most effective means of eliminating 11 million human beings. Should they use shooting, carbon monoxide, poison gas, burning etc. There are jokes, a bit of flirting, inter-office memos, some jockying for position. Other than the agenda, one would feel that he were attending the regular Board meeting of any contemporary organization. "Other than the agenda!!" Humans can only have such an agenda when they are not, in their own minds, discussing other human beings, but "things". It is deceptively easy for us to "thingify" others - "foreigners", "pakis", "heathens' etc. and forget their humaness.

The message of Philemon rings through the ages. No person is a a statistic. Every man woman and child is a loved one of God.

Prayer

Great God of all life and all people, we come rejoicing that you have given us life and love, but also responsibility, for passing these on to those we meet. We ask your strength and your gentleness, that we may grow in wisdom and in humility, in bravery and in tenderness, in vision and in practical sense, as we support all who are "put down" by others, because of their land of birth, the colour of their skins, their lack of education or of income. May we remember always that each person we meet is a child of your love. Amen.

Notes on use of this service, including dates, occasions and possible changes.

Blameless

Call

O God, you are our God. Early will we seek you. Our souls thirst for you, long for you, as in a dry and thirsty land where no water is.

Prayer

Have mercy upon us, O God, according to your loving-kindness; according to the multitude of your tender mercies, blot out our transgressions. Wash us and clean us, for our sins are ever before us. Create in us, clean hearts, O god, and renew a right spirit within us. O Lord, open our lips that our mouths may shout forth your praise. Amen.

Scripture Reading

Psalm 119:1-8
Matthew 5: 17-24

Suggested Hymns

31 (suggested alternate tune 263)
63 (suggested alternate tune 430)

Please use your imaginations today. Imagine Jesus sitting in the synagogue on the Sabbath. His mother sits on the opposite side, amongst the women. Jesus watches her now and then as he thinks of what is being read. Joseph has been dead some years, and although Jesus, the eldest male, is the head of the household, Mary remains a powerfully significant figure in the life of the family.

A Psalm is being chanted now. "Blessed are those whose way is blameless, who walk in the way of the Lord." It is the longest Psalm in the collection and is a bit of a literary curiosity being an "acrostic" - that is, the opening letters of each of the 22 stanzas follow the Hebrew alphabet, we would say from A to Z. Also, each of the 172 verses uses the name of God in some way. It is a God-saturated song of adoration. As a literary form it is a trifle artificial but the Hewbrew writers liked that kind of thing. A Scottish commentator noting both its monotony and its power wrote, "It is like a master violinist playing a work on only one string". More significant is its understanding of the nature of God and humanity.

Jesus had heard this psalm countless times. Before memory he had heard it at his mother's knee. He thinks of her now as the familiar words roll over him. She sits across the synagogue, serene yet strong, like the Psalm itself.

Thirty years earlier Mary had sung the Magnificat. "My soul magnifies the Lord. From henceforth all generations shall call me blessed." Strange words for this hard-working widow in little Nazareth. She had not yet come to the place where all would call her blessed, but nor had she come to the place predicted by old Simeon who, at Jesus' dedication, had said to her, "And a sword shall pierce your soul also." She sits in the synagogue quietly certain that both pain and blessing are yet to come. Meanwhile she returns the knowing smile of her son and each turns again to the Psalm.

"Blessed are those who walk in the way

of the Lord". Jesus had spent thirty years reflecting on the way of the Lord. He had saturated himself in the Psalms and their assurance about those who walked in God's ways. He was now close to the time when he must leave home and take a new role. His mind went out to the the crowds who would soon enjoy the remainder of the Sabbath sitting at home or on the hillside near the town discussing the scriptures. He imagined himself speaking to them about the way of the Lord.

Then his mind went to the words, "Blessed are those whose way is blameless." How could one account himself or herself blameless? Who was blameless?

Was his mother? He looked across the room again. Thoughts crowded into his mind. Thoughts of a search for a lost coin, of lighting a candle to give light to the house, of the yeast at work in the ·dough, of the forgiving parent. Here was one who was as blameless as any person could be. Yet she must experience some feeling of failure. Fine-tuned as she was to God's will, responding to the spirit as a reflex responds to touch, was she blameless?

No one could be totally righteous, he knew. It was not possible to keep the law perfectly. He thought of how his mother at Passover would take the family to Jerusalem. They would stay with her parents near the pool of Bethesda, only steps from the Temple. As the eldest son, after consulting with his mother, Jesus would go to the temple to purchase the sacrificial animal. He thought of how the family would lay hands on the doves, purchased at a cost they would feel for some time. They would feel the release of all guilt as the blood flowed on

the altar - the gift of life returned to the giver - and then, in turn, given back to them as the blood was sprinkled on their garments to indicate the cleansing mercy of God. All could stand blameless, then, knowing that their cleansing was a gift of God, not the result of their own effort or merit. If only once, they could have afforded a lamb! But Mary had assured them, God understands, God will provide.

Prayer

Cleanse us, O Lord, with your wondrous forgiveness. For we know our need, and know our own helplessness. Yet we know also the love that Jesus has brought. May it bless us now. Then may we give time and talent, treasure and testimony, to telling the world the wondrous story of your love. May we speak not just with our mouths but in our actions, always. Amen.

Notes on use of this service, including dates, occasions and possible changes.

Run with Courage

O Give thanks to the Lord, for he is good; for his steadfast love endures for ever.

Prayer

Lord of the wide earth and the open sky, Lord of all fruitful silence, we lift our hearts that we may see beyond the narrow limits of our words and habits. Prepare us, by the wonder of your mighty gifts, stars and seas, mountains and rivers, flowers and fertility, to discern your presence in all the world and in all inner lovliness, that we may find within and without the endless mercy, wisdom and courage that you offer always, in Jesus name. Amen.

Scripture Reading

1st Corinthians 9:19-27
Hebrews 12:1-4

Suggested Hymns

166 175

Summer brings summer games, whether it be the Olympics, Commonwealth Games, or local meets. Paul would have loved it.

Most people probably do not think of the Apostle Paul as a sports buff, but he was. He grew up in Tarsis, which he described as "no mean city". In fact, Tarsis had a lot going for it, but one of its chief claims to fame was that it was the site of the Cilician Games, a semi-final trial for the Olympics. One can imagine the city after the games, youngsters in every street and backlot imitating the runners, the jumpers, the weight lifters, the boxers. Paul would certainly have been one of them.

In one of his best loved passages Paul described life as a huge track meet in which each has an assigned event, and the stands are filled by those who have completed their races and now cheer us on. This is his picture of the communion of saints.

Throughout his writings Paul used coloquial terms that would be known only to sports fans. Most grandmothers would not be able to decode the headline *Gretsky pulls Hat trick*, but every hockey fan can. Paul used sports-page terms just as puzzling for many people as that one. For, example, when Paul wrote, "I subdue my body" he actually wrote "I deliver a knock out blow to my body. I K.O. my body"!!

Paul believed that the Christian life required a spirit and body as well disciplined as that of a top athlete. He knew that bodies that are not given sufficient training go soft. So do spirits, and wills, and even feelings. "Do not become weary in well doing", he cautioned, perhaps thinking of teams he had watched who "faded in the clutch", who could not keep up the pace. In the gruelling pace of international hockey it is often the final period that really counts because the team that is in the best "condition" can often surpass a team that is wilting. Paul was a spiritual athlete and urged his friends to follow his example.

Training is neccessary for the inner struggle, the battle with temptation and self-indulgence. Browning wrote, "When the fight begins within a man, then he is worth something." Life is a battle, an inner contest with forces that would have us give up on caring for others or for God. William James writes:

> If this life is not a real fight, in which something is eternally gained for the universe by success, then it is not better than a game of charades from which one can withdraw at will. But it feels like a fight, as if there were something wild in the universe which we must wrestle and subdue.

That is Paul's kind of language.

Church members often feel that confirmation is the end of their training period. Any athlete who thinks that when she is finished her initial training she is ready to compete for the gold would be laughed out of the locker room. In his last years, writing to his friends in Phillipi from jail in Rome Paul used another sports term. "Forgetting the things that are past", he wrote, "I press on towards the goal". That phrase "press on towards the goal" is all caught up in one single and unusual Greek word - epekteinomenos- a familiar picture, the racer going hard for the finish line, clawing the air, with body thrusting to the tape. That was Paul's spirit, driving all the way, and it is the spirit he suggests for all Christians.

Prayer

Our God, the seasons turn, and each turning brings us fresh prospects for living and loving. We are grateful for the coming of summer. We are surrounded by beauty on every side as roses bloom, golden wheat waves, buffalo beans and tiger lilies brighten the roadside, trillum and shooting stars peep from beneath shade trees, leafy branches meet across the streets, blues deepen and shimmer in sky and water. We thank you for the pause in our daily routine, school vacations, holidays from work, the change of pace that brings refreshment to body and mind. We are grateful for opportunities to travel, for family reunions and the renewal of friendships, for fresh growth and learning in a season of unusual experiences. In our joy we would stay aware of the needs of others. We pray for those who see roses only in the windows of the corner florist shop. Those whose streets are not shaded by green trees but only reflect the glare of sun on pavement. Those who must see and read of others enjoying summer recreation while for them summer brings only problems of unatttended children and steamy days at work. For these we pray, in Jesus' name. Amen.

Notes on use of this service, including dates, occasions and possible changes.

Dungeons in the Air

Call

Make a joyful noise unto the Lord. Come into his courts with thanksgiving and into his presence with rejoicing.

Prayer

Great God, you were the first word sounding in the silence of creation; you were the light moving over the dark waters; you were the deep urge that brought order out of chaos; you were the sculptor of human life. So are you still, creator, mover, enlightener, shaper. We would thank you, and would bend our will to your molding now, in Christ our Lord. Amen.

Scripture Reading

2nd Corinthians 4:8-16

Suggested Hymns

34, 197

The still popular pop-psychology book, *Games People Play*, by Eric Berne can make us quite uncomfortable - overexposed. He describes a lot of human behaviour as "games". As we read we all realize what game-players we are. Cruel behaviour is often made socially acceptable when practised in playful forms. The behaviour Berne describes can also be harmful to ourselves. The games we play tend to confirm us in our bad habits and our willingess to put ourselves down.

A frequent game is one he calls, "Aint It Awful". It reduces all of life to "not OK". It hints at a kind of malevolence behind life that colours it all grey, if not

black. "Well, that's the way things go", "Isn't it always the way". The weather, the younger generation, the Middle East - all are assigned to an unpleasant, unchanging shade of drab.

A generation or two ago parents used to warn children about "building castles in the air" - being unduly optimistic or hopeful. A more common pastime now is building "dungeons in the air", mocking life. Building dungeons in the air puts life down. One could spend a day compiling common phrases that suggest the hopelessness of life - "Back to the salt mine, " "unholy deadlock", "You can't buck city hall" and so on. "Ain't it Awful". A grey mood settles over the soul like spent ashes. Nothing seems worthwhile, no one seems good, all expressions of hope or enthusiasm sound old-fashioned or phoney.

Playwright,Tennessee Williams captured the mood with great sensitivity.

The moment after the phone has been hung up, the hand reaches for the scratch pad and scrawls "Funeral, Tue, 5:00, Holy Redeemer - flowers" and the same hand is only a little shakier as it reaches for a highball glass that will pour a stupefecation over the kindled nerves... so we have disguised from ourselves the intensity of our feelings, the sensibility of our hearts.

Why do we hide our feelings, even from ourselves? It is something we learn. A cynical child is unthinkable. A young person may "play it cool" but that kind of cynicism is a healthy stage in development. Peanuts cartoons often say it all. In one, cranky Lucy tells Charlie Brown she is going to be a political cartoonist, "I'm going to ridicule everything". Charlie Brown responds. "I understand, Lucy. By the use of ridicule you hope to point out the faults of government and thus improve our way of life." Lucy shouts. "No, you idiot, I just want to ridicule everything!" There is a healthy dose of both Lucy and Charlie Brown in youthful cyncism.

But when that sort of cynicism continues into adulthood it indicates arrested development. It can result in a permanent grudge against life, a drawn out quarrel with the values of humanity.

Displaced cynicism can be detected now in many forms - in stale immorality that masquerades as daring liberation; in sick satire and black humour in the media; in a lack of volunteers for service; in the distrust of the process of law and government; in a lack of leaders who care for anything but their own gain; in listless responses to causes that truly matter.

Cynicism is a subtle sin. It does not use frontal attack. It nibbles away at the soul. Our spirits become diminished and tattered before we know what has happened. Age wrinkles the face, but cynicism wrinkles the soul.

Cynicism is attractive because it is easier to live with than faith is. In another Peanuts strip, Sally, the baby sister of Lucy and Linus is crawling about. Linus asks, How long do you think it will be before Sally learns to walk?" Lucy shouts, (she always shouts), "Good grief, what's the hurry? Let her crawl for a while. Don't rush her. Once you stand up and walk you're committed for life."!!

In the scripture reading today Paul is dealing with this problem. "Take no part in the unfruitful works of darkness. Awake, O sleeper, and rise from the dead, and Christ shall give you light." The death of which Paul writes is a lack of vision, of purpose. We are preserved from such death by our faith.

Prayer

Lord God, it is so easy to be seduced by the cool and the catty. It seems clever to be world-weary. It is harder to trust life with our hopes and dreams. It is easier to hide them under laughter and ridicule. Keep us honest with our own hearts, O God. Help us to face our best selves without shame, that we may then face the world with hopes held high and with pride in our dreams. Amen.

Notes on use of this service, including dates, occasions and possible changes.

Rock and Refuge

Call
He who dwells in the shelter of the Most High, who abides in the shadow of the Almighty, will say to the Lord, "My refuge and my fortress; my God, in whom I trust."

Prayer
Lord of all power and might, maker and giver of all good things, we scan our days for signs of your presence and the week behind for the assurance of your love. We need your strength, the shelter of your loving care, the refreshment of a quiet time in your presence. So we come, and so we pray, that we may joined to one another and to your spirit. May this time be for reflection and for learning, for peace and for power. In Jesus name, Amen.

Scripture Reading
Psalm 46   Romans 8:28-39

Suggested Hymns
134   79

The imagery of Psalm 436 echoes throughout the Bible. The land where the Bible was composed was scorching, much of the time. The rock was an essential source of shelter where there was often no other. It provided so much security for the sun-soaked wanderer that this nomad people spoke of God as a rock.

"The Rock - his work is perfect and whole. All his ways are justice."

Today we feel some ambivalence with this imagery. Some feel felt God has become a shelter from reality, a hiding place for those too weak to fend for themselves. Church people, they say, might better spend their time in training for life's battle than in singing to the Rock of Ages.

Though religion can become a retreat from responsibility, there are times when a retreat is essential. The "rock" is a good image for such times. Rock has about it that feeling of "from everlasting to everlasting".

Naturalists tell us that when the wind comes up and a honeybee is unable to maintain its flight it will cling to a rock until the wind subsides. In the swaying, swirling, sweep of change, there are times when each of us must simply hold on.

The Psalmist had more in mind. There is a second way of translating the words from the original Hebrew. They can be translated, as we are accustomed to do, "... safe to the rock that is higher than I" - with its fine sense of security. They can also be translated, "safe to the rock that it too high for me". We are expected to reach beyond the boundaries of familar competence. We are expected to stretch, so the rock becomes, rather than a refuge, a challenge. So God is to be found in both the calm and the climb.

In either case we have the asurance that we are not left at the mercy of our own unaided efforts.

Psalm 46 was written in response to a well known historic event, the seige of Jerusalem by Assyrian troops. Some will remember reading in English class Byron's powerful poem that starts,

The Assyrian came down like a wolf on the fold
And his cohorts were gleaming in purple and gold,
And the sheen of his spears was like stars on the sea
When the blue waves roll nightly on deep Galilee.

The Assyrian army was a mighty force. All seemed hopeless! Suddenly the invading army was decimated by illness. The Bible reports, "That night the angel of the Lord went forth and slew a hundred and eighty-five thousand in the camp of the Assyrians.

Byron writes,

And the might of the Gentile, unsmote by the sword,
Hath melted like snow in the glance of the Lord.

Historians suspect a plague, armies camping under unsanitary conditions were subject to typhus, bubonic plague and other disasters. Who knows? Out of the experience came the Psalm, "God is our refuge and our strength; a very present help in trouble."

Ever since it has been a song of hope for those in desperate circumstance. Luther spoke often of the miraculous relief from the seige of Leipzig, and, in fact, compared it to the way the devil had laid seige to his own life. His reliance on Psalm 46 as a source of hope in dark days resulted in his most famous hymn, a poetic version of the psalm.

A safe stronghold our God is still.

Martin Luther King drew strength from it the night he made his decision to fight for black rights despite his natural inclination to a quiet life of scholarship and pastoral care. Years later he would cry out, "I have a dream - and I got it at the rock."

We are not a desert people for whom the rock is a welcome shelter, nor medieval Christians threatened by a seiging pagan army, nor are we having to make dramatic decisions about our lives. But we have our own kinds of stress. We must deal with headlines of homicides, production deadlines, or family ultimatums. In a lesser way we must cope with mail carriers who will not carry and flight attendants who will not attend, with traffic and toilets that jam, and with frightening drives within that threaten to destroy the fabric of our lives. God will continually challenge, but Godf also remains our rock and refuge.

Prayer

Lord God, our fortress, our rock, our refuge, our strength and our stay, hear our prayer, be our guard while troubles last. Yet move us from the shelter to serve in the heat of the day, and when the day is over may we find in you our eternal home. Amen

Notes on use of this service, including dates, occasions and possible changes.

Lent - Ash Wednesday

Call

Have mercy on us, O God, according to your steadfast love; according to your abundant mercy, blot out our transgressions.

Prayer

O Lord God, Maker of all things, Lover of all persons, Judge of all nations, we praise your name and rejoice in your presence. You are the beginning and the end of days. Without you we are as nothing, lost and lone, drifting and despairing. With you we have confidence and hope. Grant us then your presence to cleanse and restore us, in Jesus name. Amen.

Scripture Reading

Mark 1:1-12

Suggested Hymns

145,   74 (suggested alternate tune 278)

Lent is a time for personal stocktaking. It is a season of humility when we recognize the limitations that impede ouor growth towardsd maturity.

Maturity could be described as the way in which, despite recognizing, our limitations, we have faith in our ability to accomplish something. We do our best, then, and leave the rest to God. This could sound like giving up, but it is, rather, a matter of coming to terms with ourselves, with ambition, with hope, with sin, with pain. Each of these is a "boundary" against which we can fight or with which we can settle.

Lent, historically, provides us with a set time for coming to terms with the limitations that life and our human existence impose on us.

We begin with the limits of .knowledge. The Christian is one who has exchanged intellectual arrogance for humility before the vastness of God's creation. Religious living begins with awe.

We have come through, a period in which awe has not been highly regfarded. That is changing. Lewis Thomas, a highly regarded writer, has for fifteen years been commenting on the science scene. His writing contains a deep sense of wonder. He calls on those who teach science courses to do so with humility.

Let it be known early that there are deep mysteries and profound paradoxes ... Let it be known that there are some things going on in the universe that lie beyond the comprehension ... Teach that there are structures squirming inside our cells providing all the energy for living, but that they are essentially foreign creatures brought in a billion or so years ago, the lineal descendants of bacteria. Teach that we do not have the ghost of an idea how they got there.

Here is humility, the basic religious posture. When Jesus described the ideal religious attitude he did not have us picture a philosopher - he took a child and set him in the midst. That is the spirit of Lent.

Lent helps us also to recognize the limitations of our own goodness. In Mary Gordon's excellent novel *Men and Angels* a leading character says, "What is good? and where is forgiveness when goodness fails? Those are the big questions" Those questions form the backbone of Lent. At the outer limit of our goodness we encounter sin. Sin is simply what occurs when the human will shoves aside the divine will. Sin is "I" above all else.

It is not a matter of performance but of presumption. It is having a false picture of our place in the world. Out of that false view of life will issue wrong acts, which may be called "sins". Again we face our limits. With the forgiveness of God acting as our power source we can, with varying degrees of success, press against the limits of our goodness. In Paul's description of good acts, we "do nothing out of selfishness or conceit but, in humility, count others more important than ourselves, looking not to our own interests, but to the interests of others."

One other limit is often examined in Lent - the limitations inherent in the fact of suffering and tragedy. The world is not put together fairly. Some seem to carry more of the burden of unfairness than others. We make peace with this fact or are burnt out throwing ourselves against it. A minister in California who losts a teen-aged daughter in a car accident wrote, "You can't unring a bell,/ You can't unshine a star,/ You can't retrieve a word you've said,/The things that are, just are."

We may rebel and scream - and we should. We may question and challenge, but eventually we sit down alongside our tragic facts, take them up in our arms, and carry them into life with us, knowing that God walks with us in all that we experience. "He that spared not his own son, will he not also give us all things with him?" Knowing this, life can be calm, and we can learn the blessing of Lent.

Prayer

Lord God, all that comes to pass comes with your presence in it. You are the way we walk, the truth we seek, the life we find . Grant us, now, imagination, clarity of purpose, a lively conscience, the helping word, the caring action, that our days may increase in usefulness to you and your children. May this season of Lent, lead us out to the frightening limits of our own abilties and strengths, but may we find there the strength of the hills that comes from you and the peace that passes all understanding, through Christ our Lord. Amen.

Notes on use of this service, including dates, occasions and possible changes.

Good Friday

Call

If we say that we have no sin we deceive ourselves and the truth is not in us; but if we confess our sins He is faithful and just to forgive and to cleanse us from all unworthiness.

Prayer

Our God, as the shadow of the cross falls across this week, bring us deeply and devoutly to consider our lives, we pray. May we present ourselves to the discipline your Holy Spirit, repenting of our sinful carelessness until,with newness of will, we return to your way. Build us into a fellowship of love and mercy that others may find among us a sanctuary of hope and strength. In Christ's name we pray. Amen.

Hymn

452 - O sacred head

Scripture Reading

Isaiah 53:4-9

Meditation

The cross reveals our sin. "Where You There" is no Good Friday cliche, but a neccessity, like Silent Night at Christmas or Christ the Lord is Risen Today at Easter. We were there. We are there.

The most startling thing about the cross is that it was the work of men and women of average or above-average goodness. Recall the faces around the cross. These people stood for law and order, church and decency. Like them, we live in a world where it is easy to be tragically wrong as we pursue our best

insights, as we follow our most trusted leaders. How cautiously we must hold opinions, how thoroughly we must examine our motives, how sternly check our prejudices. The best of people, not the worst, nailed him there. Jesus knew it. "They know not what they do".

Observe a time of silence

Prayer

Help us, O God, in this season of penitence and honesty to recognize how easily our lives are possessed and twisted by unworthy motives masquerading as the good. Keep our hearts and spirits vigilant lest we find ourselves among your enemies. In the name of Christ we pray, Amen.

Hymn 174

Scripture Reading

Luke 23:33-38

Meditation

Luke provides a factual account of an historic event.

Crucifixion was a cruel and spectacular method of execution that the Romans had taken over from the Carthaginians. The victims outstretched arms were nailed or tied to the crossbeam, and then this plank was nailed or tied to a vertical pole. Sometimes a projection was nailed below the feet to give some support to the near naked body. The feet were tied or nailed. Death was usually the result of slow exhaustion rather than loss of blood.

So Jesus died.

It is not that the physical sufferings of Jesus were more shocking than those experienced by many victims of cruelty, then and now, but that this could be done to one who embodied the very goodness of God. Our recognition of the depth of God's love is found in the facts of Christ's death. So is our recognition of the depth of human resistance to that love.

Our Christian faith is not a set of arguments about the existence or nature of God. It is the record of the dynamic self-disclosure and self-giving of the living God in the events of human history. Those events have a time and place. The central claim is not that God is, but that God acts. The Eternal God is in active, personal, redeeming contact with the word. The proper posture before such incredible news is to kneel in humble joy.

Palgrave, in his diary, tells of being in Paris in 1848. The Tuilleries were being wrecked by the mob. They broke into the chapel, and stopped before a painting of the crucifix. "Bare your heads", one said. They did. They knelt, They carried the picture out in silence. "You might have heard a fly buzz," reports Palgrave. Then the wave of destruction rolled on. God's Good Friday action still stops us in our tracks.

John Milton wrote a lovely poem *An Ode on the Morning of Christ's Nativity.* He planned to do a companion piece on the death of Jesus. He wrote a few lines but laid it aside with the comment. "This subject, the author finding to be above the years he had when he wrote it, and nothing satisfied with what was begun,

left it unfinished." Before God's love, we are silenced.

Observe a time of silence.

Prayer
Almighty God, there are mysteries beyond us in your word. Our minds and hearts have not yet plumbed them. There are heights that we have not dared to climb, and depths we have feared to descend. We feel all of these as we stand before the cross of Jesus. We sense that our true salvation lies here. We feel the world's pain in the shadow of the cross. We catch a glimpse of your own pain in the darkness at noon. May we stand bravely in the midst of its mystery until we feel, in your presence, a strength that rises above the pain. May we feel your love reaching out from the shadows to renew us and set us on our way with confidence and joy, in Christ's name. Amen.

Notes on use of this service, including dates, occasions and possible changes.

Annual Meeting

Call

Oh people of God, hope in the Lord, from this time forth and forevermore.

Prayer

Lord of all days, we thank you for time to reflect. We would look backwards now, over the year behind us, to find there evidence of your leading. We would look ahead, confident that you will provide work for our hands and heads. We are grateful for the friendships that grow up between us as we work and worship together, and pray that you will use the life of our group to fulfill the purposes of your Kingdom here. Speak to us now - through song and scripture, through the words of friends, through your own inner voice speaking silently in our hearts, through the very presence of the risen Christ in our midst, that our reflecting and our planning may be to your glory, for we ask it in the name of Jesus. Amen.

Scripture Reading

Genesis 28:10-16   Acts 16:6-10

Suggested Hymns

223,   152

"I have a dream". It is many years now since Martin Luther King Jr. stood at the Washington Monument and delivered those words, but they will never be forgotten. Whenever a man or a woman says, "I have a dream" the whole world waits and listens.

At this annual meeting our minds may well go to those whose dreams were responsible for the founding of our church or of this group. ((You may, at this point, wish to add some local data appropriate to these thoughts)). Those builders exemplify Plato's advice. "Have a dream; have a great dream; dream it greatly." They built on a firm foundation laid at the beginnings of our faith.

The Bible puts a good deal of stock in dreaming. We sing of Jacob's ladder, his dream that there was an unfailing connection between heaven and earth. The early church bridged from Asia to Europe following Paul's dream of a man calling him over to preach the gospel there.

It is strange that we should use the term "dreamer" for someone who is impractical and non-productive, because it is the dreamers who get things done. The dreamer is the builder, the shaper.

We are the music makers, and we are the dreamers of dreams,
> Wandering by lone sea-breakers,
> And sitting by desolate streams.
> World-losers and world forsakers
> On whom the pale moon gleams:
> Yet we are the movers and shaker
> Of the world, forever, it seems.

Now, as we come to our annual meeting, we look to the year ahead, and beyond. It is a good time to ask, "Just what are our dreams for our church?" Howard Thurman used to say, "Where there is no dream life becomes a swamp, a dreary dead place and deep within the heart

---

114

begins to rot." This can happen to a church. So, what shape do our dreams take? Many of them will be contained in the reports of executive and committees. Let us take time to define carefully what our vision of the future may be.

When we have taken a careful look at our plans, our dreams, we will want to ask ourselves, "Would Jesus be pleased with these dreams.?" Would we be proud to sit on our patios or in our living rooms in front of the fireplace tonight and share them with him? Is there enough here to tax our talents? to stretch us? Are they the dreams of a group committed to love for neighbour? Remember the poular words from *Sound of Music.* "Climb every mountain, ford every stream, follow every rainbow, till you find your dream." Do they have this kind of challenge in them?

Are we willing to risk to make it come true? Every good dream issues in action. We mentioned Jacob's ladder. That dream came as a surprise to Jacob. He actually thought he had escaped from God but the dream forced him to see that God was everywhere. On that basis he built an altar, returned home, made amends, and changed his ways. Following a dream can be costly. It can also be magnetic. Howard Thurman says two miracles are attached to dreaming. One, the dreamer becomes her dream. Two, the dream begins to exert a pull on others.

One of literature's great dreamers has come alive on the stage with *The Man of La Mancha.* Don Quixote's song sums up the best dreams of humankind.((If possible have a soloist sing the song. Otherwise, the words can be read))

To dream the impossible dream, to fight the unbeatable foe,
To bear the unbearable sorrow,
To run where the brave dare not go,
To right the unrightable wrong,
To try when your arms are too weary,
To reach the unreachable star.

It is a long way from the dream to the drudgery of making it come true, but it is the way God has chosen for his children to live - from dream to action, from action to accomplishment.

Prayer
O God, you have honoured us by calling us into your church. In that calling you have promised to be our guide and our strength. As we look ahead we are deeply aware of our need of your presence. The tasks are large and the volunteers few. It is easy for us to become weary, cynical, and finally bitter. Yet we would keep our eyes on Jesus whose loving spirit did not fail him even on the cross. Grant us his vision, we pray. Amen.

Notes on use of this service, including dates, occasions and possible changes.

A Celebration of Families

((For use in family retreat, open air family service, camp etc.))

Call

This is the day that the Lord has made. Let us rejoice and be glad in it.

Prayer

Our loving God, we would be building, - building lives, building homes, building families, building communties, building our nation, but we know that unless you, the Lord, build the house, we labour in vain when we build. As we consider our life together, open our eyes to new insights into life; open our minds to new ideas; and open our hearts to a new love for all who are your children and our family. In Jesus' name. Amen.

Scripture Reading

Joshua 24:13-15   lst John 4:7-12

Suggested Hymns

199,   197

Some children have alphabet books. Probably some have one that says, A is for Apple. If you are a little older it may say A is for Aardvark. They get harder as you go along.

What might B be for? ((answers like "bugle, boy, ball etc)). C could be candle or cauliflower. Today we would probably all agree that F is for Family.Its good to be together with our families thinking together about what is important for us.

F could also be for FUN. Sometimes when we get together in church there's not much fun to be seen, but fun belongs in times like this. Jesus enjoyed family gatherings, banquets,wedding parties, and games. In fact, he said, I come that your joy might be full." At a gathering like this one a young fellow made up his first poem. It simply went, "Kris, Mom; Kris, Mom. Happy, happy, happy.".

The first thing the Bible tells us about God is that he made the world, and that when he was finished he said, "This is good!! It might have said, "This is good fun." Surely God had a good time making the world.

Fun is best when it is shared. In *The House at Pooh Corner* which some of you have read, Christopher Robin and Pooh Bear had a talk about fun. Christopher Robin asked Pooh what he liked doing the very best in the world.

"Well", said Pooh, "what I like best..." and then he had to stop and think. Because although eating honey was a very good thing to do,there was a moment just before you began to eat it which was better than when you were, but he didn't know what it was called. And then he thought that being with Christopher Robin was a very good thing to do, and having Piglet near was a very friendly thing to have. And so when he thought it all out he said, "What I like best in the world is me and Piglet going to see you, and you saying 'What about a little something' and me saying, 'Well, I shouldn't mind a lilttle something, should you Piglet' and it being a hummy sort of day outside and birds singing."

That does sound like fun. One man was writing a paper on things that are important to children, but that parents might not understand. He told his eight year old son what he was doing and the son said, "Children like to play all sorts of games. They like silly things that parents don't understand. The parents tell them not to do it, and the children go out and do it where the parents can't find out. And that's why parents think that there is a mystery." It sounds like some children could teach some parents how to play.

F is also for FUND. A fund is a supply of something that can be given out when needed. We usually think of money, but we can have a fund of talents too. Real love is helping the other person to find his or her talents and abilties. Helping the other person to be himself or herself. Parents are expected to have a fund of understanding and care for their children but children can also, with love and understanding help their parents to grow.

Ogden Nash writes a funny story-poem about the wrong kind of love.It starts out "Once upon a time there was a man named Orlando Tregennis, and he was in love with his wife (he thought)." In order to have his wife give him "a look of love" he climbed the highest mountain in the world and named it after her. But, Nash tells us,
"She didn't give him a look of love, she gave him a look of laughter.
And not only a look of laughter but a look of menace.
Because he named it after his wife by naming it

Mount Mrs. Orlando Tregennis."

Much so-called loving of others, even in the family, is really loving ourselves, but using other people to do it.

F is also for Fundamental. That is a big word that means "at the foundation". The foundation is the solid rock or concrete that a house is built on. Jesus reminded us often that our lives have to be built on a solid base. An old lady, over 90, told her minister, "What I learned at my mother's knee is still best." That's where we hear the stories that stay with us all our lives. Thats often where foundations are laid. Fun, funding, foundation - these words remind us of three ways that families grow together as God intended them to do.

Prayer
Dear God, we are met in families today. We know that we often make one another tense and even angry, yet we know that we can also make one another joyful and proud. May we help one another to grow in Jesus' way. Amen.

Notes on use of this service, including dates, occasions and possible changes.